White L

Thanks for your support!
Very best wishes,

Billy

Billy McCourt

© Billy McCourt, 2011

Published by William McCourt

A CIP catalogue record for this book is available from the British Library.

ISBN 978-0-9571227-0-3

Prepared and printed by:

York Publishing Services Ltd
64 Hallfield Road
Layerthorpe
York YO31 7ZQ
Tel: 01904 431213

Website: www.yps-publishing.co.uk

The Prologue.

"And now the Prologue!"

Do you remember Frankie Howard? If you do, it's a fair bet that you could be about my age, a fifties baby, a child of the sixties, or maybe it's possible that you're one of the thousands of Nineties students who adopted Frankie as the ultimate gay icon. If you're none of these, you're probably wondering, "Who the hell is Frankie Howard?" And if you have heard the name before, it's reasonable to think "What has a raving queer got to do with all this?

I should explain.

Amongst many other things, Frankie Howard was a very camp stand-up comedian, who, back in the sixties, used to introduce and star in a TV program called "Up Pompeii", and with the words, "And now the Prologue....", he began the show.

Now, before you get started, I need to point out right away, that it was easy to spot gay men in those days, because they had high pitched voices, went "ooooo", a lot, and called each other "ducky". Or so I thought?
Try and think on that this was before "Brokeback Mountain" made being gay a trendy pastime, and *no I didn't watched it because I have leanings towards the homosexual community...no sir, and for the record , I'm not homophobic either!*
No, there were no Julian Clarys or Graham Nortons on the estate where I grew up, all those years ago, The poor buggers, no pun intended, wouldn't have lasted five minutes, not with the bunch of hard nosed miner's kids who lived there, and isn't it weird how it's fashionable to be camp nowadays, but totally not politically correct to outwardly express appreciation for the female form.

Anyhow, the only reason I watched "Up Pompeii " was because, to a young and impressionable teenage boy, *it was the nearest thing to sex, in real life, or even on the TV, I ever saw*.

We had a very poor diet in those days, *and this was way before Sam Fox got her boobs out on page three*.

"Up Pompeii", and the occasional, "Health and Efficiency" magazine, showing overweight naked German women playing volleyball were about all we could look forward to, and ever since then, the words, "…and now the prologue..", throws into my mind, the image of the very sexy and very lovely Madeleine Smith, romping around a T.V. screen in a short skimpy, and very sexy toga, alongside other such lovelies in similar erotic attire. It was a program full of outrageous, boundary pushing innuendos.

When I look back now, I cringe.

But Madelaine Smith was really, really, gorgeous, and no, I'm not homophobic!

The world has changed since then.

In the non politically correct world of the 1960's and 1970's, which were I suppose my real formative years, it was allowed to think like this. It wasn't sexist, in fact there was no such thing as being sexist….honest! Ogling at women was a perfectly natural pastime. and we were positively encouraged to be like this.

"Life on Mars", that brilliant T.V. series, is, seriously, a piece of real life history.

It was all around us!

Our role models were Sean Connery as James Bond, with a gorgeous girl on each arm, and Elvis draped in Hawaiian beauties. Women were beautiful creatures who we could whistle at, if we had the confidence, and who, more often than not, enjoyed the appreciation and smiled back. Ladies, that awful awful derisive term, were there to be looked at longingly, put on pedestals to worship, to be romanced, treasured and cared for, and a beautiful woman back then wasn't something to be scared of or ignored.

I've started to ramble. I suppose what I'm really trying to say is that the world has changed a great deal since I was testosterone charged teenager, in many ways for the better. But I still adore women, and am proud to admit it!
Yes, the world has changed.

To get to the point, my world changed even more yesterday, because I was told I've got Cancer, and I'm now going to need a major operation to remove it…. Bummer!

All a bit of a shock really, and, it's fair to admit, I'm a little confused. I suppose some part of me is in a kind of state of denial, and is a little scared of what's going to happen next.

It sort of explains my ramblings.

All because of a six letter word beginning with C, my life has gone a little bit pear shaped. The only other six letter word in the English Language that begins with C and causes me emotional distress is Celery. but that's another story.

This, I suppose, is "My Prologue".

Yesterday, I got a bit of a shock.
I went to The Royal Orthopedic Hospital, a top cancer hospital in Birmingham, where the Consultant, a bloke called Rob

Grimer, said something like, "You've got Cancer", and, "it's the good kind of Cancer", and something along the lines of, "If you're going to get Cancer, this is the best one to get." He also said it's a type of Cancer that grows very slowly, something called a Chondrosarchoma, and it doesn't respond to treatment......and there I was, drip white for the second time that day, putting on a brave face, and not a very happy pixie.

He then said something like, "With luck, and because we've caught it early, and once we've operated to remove it, it's fairly certain the cancer will be gone forever.".... and through the fog, I picked up on a glimmer of good news. Was it light at the end of the tunnel maybe?

"It'll mean removing half your pelvis, hip, and the top of the femur, and, Oh yes, the next job will then be to replace what I can only be considered a sizeable chunk of my body, with about £10,000's worth of Titanium!"...Ok, not so good news, seriously wazzed off, and by now there was a maelstrom of emotions whirling about inside my head.

But hey, it can't be all bad can it?

I felt it important to grab hold of something positive quick before I went under, and the best I came up with was, *"It worked for Steve Austin, in "The Six Million Dollar Man"...... I suppose it could be worse"*.
So, here I am, an hour later, driving up the M6, having spent the best part of an hour trying to make some real sense of this little bombshell, and, believe it or not, while trying to put my very confused thoughts into some kind of order, *I had an epiphany.*

I would write a book.

4

It seems, at this moment, like such a good idea.

Anyhow, let me fill you in on some background stuff, and how things got to where we are today, because surprisingly, for some unfathomable reason, my thinking is all of a sudden a lot sharper than it was yesterday, and over the past twenty four hours, I've worked out that the "writing a book and ranting at a computer screen" thing, will keep me busy and help take my mind off other more pressing matters.

Seriously though, at this moment in time, I'm not even sure if I've anything that's worth writing about or if the whole idea isn't just a little bit arrogant and a little bit silly, but for the record, I have a GCE in English, and have, in some ways, spent most of my life telling stories.

So I thought, "Why not tell my own little tale!"? It just seems like a good idea right now.

Or am I just confused and panicking? I mean, my whole life has been turned on its' head with this little piece of news, and the whole concept of any time I've got left on the planet, indeed, my very mortality, has taken on a whole new meaning. I am about to embark on a sort of journey and I don't know exactly where this journey is going to take me, or how long it's going to take, *but if I'm honest with myself, and I am trying to be, a very big part of what my life to date has been a sort of," Let's follow the thread, and see where we end up", sort of life.*

I thought I'd call the book, "My Cancer, and how I got rid of it in thirty days! ", but this seemed a bit flippant and would sort of demean what is a fairly serious event in most people's lives.

Instead, I've decided to call it "Just Billy", just because it was my kid's idea. (I was going to call it "White Lycra Man", but they talked me out of it. I'll tell you why later.)

So, I'd better begin with how we got to where we are today.

This is my story about my Cancer, and I suppose my tale really started way back in October 2006, when it was time to start running again.

Overweight people usually go on diets. I tend to go running when I get fat because it's better than eating celery, *(Begins with a c….six letters…get it?….clever eh?)*, and this sweating like a pig regime has been a necessary activity of mine for a few years now. I've grown to love it, and like most runners, and I use the word "running" in its' broadest sense, I genuinely consider myself an athlete, even though I'm a big fat overweight bloke, *but only on the outside.* On the inside, like all men, I'm still the ultimate sex god!

I've gotten used to the questioning looks I see in the eyes of people I pass in the street, which seems to say,
" Why do they do it? "
To the uninitiated, Joggers always look in pain, and although they might see a fat bloke in Lycra, struggling along in abject misery, what they just don't realize is that that fat bloke is seeing is a different picture altogether. In his head, as in mine, he's sleek, he's athletic and smiling, and doing four minute miles.

It's his fantasy world, it's my fantasy world, and it's allowed.

I'm not a fanatic about it though, and have never had a serious scientific outlook where training is concerned, but I do have all the gadgets; Heart Rate Monitors, Pedometers, and all the technologically superior wind proof and waterproof garments that have ever been produced.

I'm a man, and I like gadgets. It's simply a man thing.

And my routine is sort of based around what could be loosely referred to as "Calendar based". By this I mean:-

I get fat at Xmas! (Doesn't everyone?)

I run and try to slim down again by Easter. (I've spent a small fortune on waterproof tops and bottoms, socks, hats, breathable underwear, in fact the whole kit and caboodle, so that whatever the weather, hail, rain or snow, I can go out running.)

I tend to fatten up again by June. (May being the start of the Barbeque season, and I do love barbeques…)

I get thinner and fitter again for August. (Because I go on holiday, and usually do some sort of a big bike ride, which usually involves cycling up a very big hill with some of my athletically confused, "Last of the Summer Wine" mates),

and then *I start to fatten up again in September.* (Probably because I get the "winter is coming blues")

I run again around November, because if I don't, I'm too out of shape by Xmas, and the next year starts even worse than the last, and the cycle continues.

Over the years, I've run in lots of 10ks, half marathons, and two London Marathons, where I was reaching the halfway stage at about the same time some anorexic stick insect was crossing the finish line. *It can't possible be healthy to be that thin, can it?*

But I particularly like getting out of bed early, and running around really nice places when the Sun is just beginning to rise. In recent times, I have done this on various beaches and mountains around the world. I also take a perverse pleasure in jogging around the monuments in some of the worlds better kept cities, getting up early and doing the tourist thing before the crowds turn up, in Paris, London, and most recently Washington D.C. where I was gently escorted off the White House grounds by a very angry security guard.

The point is, I like running.

What doesn't help is that I also love food, which has a tendency to bugger things up a little in the "looking like a Greek God" department. I've tried to change my appalling habits, honestly, but diet food just doesn't taste the same does it? And who in their right mind can enjoy skimmed milk? The creamier the sauce is, the thicker the butter, the better I like it.

So, when November came around again in 2006, it's was time to start running again, and of course, I continue to use the word running in its most flexible sense.
But this year, something was wrong.

It hurt. (It always hurt every time I started running again after a lay off, and I'd learned to expect this and run through it, but this time it was different.) But it wasn't the sort of familiar pain I knew would eventually wear off as time went by.
It was something very different.

So I stopped running, and hoped it would go away.

This January, when after the festivities I'd got fat again, I started to try running… again. The pain still hadn't gone away, and what was worse was that I sort of hit a wall, lost all energy, and physically dropped like a ton of bricks with what my G.P. termed as"Post Viral Fatigue Syndrome". *I've since learned that this a phrase used by the medical profession when they haven't a clue what the hell's wrong with you!*

I started sleeping the clock round.

My hip still hurt, so I went to the Physiotherapist, David (who I believe was thrown out of the Gestapo for cruelty), who put me through hell, smiling serenely to himself throughout. When I first met David, his opening gambit were the words, "Be prepared for pain, I've had Nuns swear at me on this table". He wasn't lying, He proceeded to tortured me relentlessly, obviously aiming to give me good value for money. But nothing seemed to get better.

Then I went to Alan, a more gentle kind of physiotherapist, who said, "Get an X-ray done, you might have arthritis." Very sound advice!

And this is where I was lucky....very very lucky!

The X-ray found something wrong, The Radiologist who found the irregularity was really on the ball because apparently, this type of tumor is incredibly difficult to diagnose and almost impossible to pick out on an X-Ray. (Something that today is very much in my favour, and I'm very grateful for.)

Then followed the tests, a CT scan, and a Nuclear Bone Scan, (which was very surreal because the instructions for the following twenty four hours were to stay away from pregnant women and small children. I mean, did they think I was some sort of perverse sex fiend, and besides I've never found pregnant women all that sexy, except of course my darling wife who may be reading this and yes my love, all the things I said to you when you were expecting were indeed true. Phew!).

9

There then followed a bone biopsy, and finally I received a phone call saying I needed to go to Birmingham for yet more tests, because something wasn't right, and we think it could be Cancer, but were not telling you just yet. As you can imagine, it was all a bit unnerving.

In honesty, I had been told very early on there was an outside chance of Cancer, but statistically, due to my age, and the lack of other symptoms, it was very unlikely. I kind of kept this very much to myself in the beginning, because there didn't seem any point in worrying anyone else needlessly. The truth was, I didn't really want to think about there being even the possibility of it being Cancer, because even the word Cancer scared me.

And the strange thing was that I felt that I was getting better.....

As time had gone by, the initial pain had almost disappeared. From a routine of taking painkillers every two hours, I'd gotten to a stage where I didn't need any at all, which I put down to being able to go out on my bike.

This bit I still find amazing.

What actually happened was that I'd gone off for a night in my campervan, and had a terrible nights' sleep, and was by now, totally sick and tired of not exercising. I was seriously missing my happy hormones which were a welcome by-product from all the jogging about I used to do.

I thought," Bugger this!", and decided to take my bike out for a ride, because anything was better than sitting around and being miserable and if it hurt, so what?
I actually only went about four miles, and enjoyed it immensely, *but strangely found that my hip felt better*.

So I did the same again the following day, *and it sorted of felt better still.* Very weird!

I kept this up for the next three weeks and got up to about seventy miles on a good day, and found that I didn't need to take the painkillers at all, so obviously, I felt that there couldn't be all that much wrong with me.....or could there?

The consultant couldn't quite understand how this was possible on a slush puppy hip,...apparently, by now, my pelvis had started to disintegrate.

Which brings us up to the present.

The final lot of tests had to be done in a specialist hospital, "The Royal Orthopedic Hospital", Birmingham, and the first half hour was really scary.

I mean, I'd never had anything like this before, never had a major operation apart from the Vasectomy. It's also worth pointing out that every bloke who has undergone this highly significant procedure has his own story to tell...and I do mean every bloke. Mine was about discovering that it's a good idea to dilute TCP before splashing it all over the man bits to help them recover when the infection sets in. The smell of burning flesh and the acrid smell of the acid fumes lingers on in my mind to this day....

It was all a bit intimidating, the hospital that is.

On arrival, I was put into a surgical ward which specialized in spinal operations, until a bed became available in the Cancer ward, and j*ust the fact that I was being admitted to a "CANCER WARD" was a big shock to the system.*

A young man was laying there in the bed opposite, and was in obvious pain. I looked over and spotted what looked like the end of a leg after it had been amputated and the hairs that started standing out on the back of my neck weren't caused by a draught from any open window. (It later turned out that all I'd spotted was his surgical stocking, but it sort of set the scene for what came next....)

Worse yet, a team of nursing staff breezed in, drew the curtains around his bed, and the words I heard next were:-

"When did you have your last bowel movement?" Bit personal I thought.

"Four days ago!" came the reply. Oh! Oh! I thought.

"We'll have to sort it out then".....a little later followed by...."Aaaaaarrrgggghhh!".

I sat there in a cold sweat, honestly believing some sort of a medieval torture implement, designed to relieve the aforementioned blockage, had been rammed up his "Torchwood" bits. (...and what's that all about anyhow, men dancing and kissing on "Doctor Who". It's not right, is it? ...sorry, I digress.)

I later found out that all they had been doing was turning him over in bed, a normal post operative activity, because unbeknown to me in my ignorance, apparently, the days of using mechanical aids to alleviate such problems were long gone.

"You haven't had one of them before, have you?", came the voice from one of the male nurses. All he'd meant was an enema, but I didn't know this, and by now I was drip white.

I'd been in the hospital for about thirty five minutes, and I don't even like needles. I was feeling like I'd been the one who'd roughly been given the laxative...if only I'd known what was to come.

After a day of Scans, CT, MRI, and more X-rays, the inevitable moment came.

"You've got a tumor!"
The words, "Oh Bugger!" came to mind. (It was probably a little different to how I describe it here, more like "Oh shit!, Oh bollocks! Or suchlike, but the gist of it is more or less the same.)

Helen went very quiet!
He had also used the word Cancer for the first time.

Now, it's reasonable to point out that the word Cancer has bowel relaxing properties in it's own right, and I remember thinking that maybe they should have whispered it into that poor bloke's ear before sticking that stuff up his...

He then gave me the worst case scenario, and didn't beat about the bush. "There's a fair chance of infection, there's a fifty-fifty chance your sex life will be affected, but that's ok because we've got little blue pills, but other than that, you will be as good as your going to get in about nine months to a years time. "

As good as you're going to get.....now what the hell does that mean??

This explains the lack of any direction during the first few days of my diary, which, if you haven't gone to sleep yet, you will hopefully begin to read shortly.... but it was obvious that for the first few days, after getting the good news, I was still in a state of shock. The Viagra thing I wasn't too worried about because Eddie, my seventy six year old father-in-law, has mentioned it briefly in passing at least *twice a day* for the past ten years, that him and Marilyn, my mother in law, are, because of the little blue pills, are going at it like…..sorry, the image something a son-in-law shouldn't have in his head…..yuk!

But, and I've totally made my mind up now….THAT IS DEFINITELY NOT GOING TO HAPPEN TO ME! ….IT'S JUST NOT… NO F…ING WAY!

Right now, and I know it sounds strange, but I'm much more worried about bowel movements! The incident with the lad and the enema had unsettled me. It might sound silly *but I never had a public school education* and therefore no-one has been anywhere near my bottom since I was a baby, and the thought of being laid flat in an hospital bed and being that dependent on somebody else worries me…..a lot.

So, where do we go from here?

What comes next then, is a sort of diary, from the moment I was told I now have Cancer, until sometime in the future, when I get back to where I've recovered if not totally, then recovered to the point where I'm as good as I'm going to get.

That bit I haven't worked out yet.

It's about my honest feelings leading up to, through, and after the operation, and how I deal with the whole Cancer thing. Maybe others deal with their Cancer in a different way, I have absolutely no idea. It's all too new!

This is how I deal with mine.

I hope that firstly, it will help me come to terms with what really is going to be a life changing experience, and secondly, someone else might take a little comfort from reading about I get through the whole thing. *The fact that I will get through it is in no doubt whatsoever.* If by reading my account, if just one person take some benefit from my experience, it'll most definitely have been worth doing.

I'm also adding stuff about me, to try and make it more upbeat, because it can't be all doom and gloom, can it?

I think I've had a blessed life, and over the years, I've had to come back from a number of ups and downs, the experiences of which I hope will help me to get through the next few months.

I've always believed that, where my life has been concerned, the journey of living it to the full has been far more important than actually reaching any destination. *Or have I just wandered aimlessly? I'm not entirely sure.* Maybe the truth is that I've just been one of life's heroic failures.

Right now, that's for others to decide.

And now seems the right time to express some heartfelt thanks, because there are a number of people who I've come across over the years who have been an obvious influence and a major contributing factor in who I am today, so there's has to be a place for them in the book, and given that I've met many weird and wonderful characters , it seems only fair I try to give them the write up they deserve.

Seriously, being told I've got Cancer has brought the whole concept of my life full into the headlights, and not for the first time. It therefore seems important to map out my little story

15

even if it's just for my kids, my close friends, and those in the family who may follow, if for no other reason.

My mortality is at this moment being questioned and I feel it's important to let the world know who I am and what made me the way I am. I might not get another chance.

My then, my now and my, "whatever comes next!".

So here goes.....

Here endeth the Prologue.

I'm just Billy, not William, but simply Billy, not what it says on my birth certificate, and surprisingly not Guillermo, which was, for many years, thought to be my name in Venezuela. .

I've always been just Billy.

My *Grandad* was called Jack, by all who knew and loved him, but his birth certificate said John. His father was John, and there has been a John is every generation as far back as I can remember, so I suppose calling him Jack was a way of telling which John was which. We have a lot of Johns in our family. Many years ago, my grandad's four sisters and brother turned up at the house once, to offer his wife, Martha, their condolences, having just heard he'd just been killed in a pit accident, only to find out it was actually his cousin who had died. He was also John McCourt.

My *father* was called Abby, but his birth certificate read Luis Armendo Rivero Cordero.

I'm just Billy.

Any why is this important you may ask?
I'll tell you why.

Names are personal things. (He's sharp this boy, I can see you thinking). They aren't just there to tell us apart. They're there to identify us to those who know us and come along with an image of what we're all about. It's like the name Hitler brings to mind an image of evil and Mercedes flags up an image of quality. I'd like to thing that Billy brings to mind dependability and humour. It's more likely to be the image of the idiot who runs around the place in the rain, getting soaked.

I taught a kid called Pete Bogg once.

I also had a college lecturer called Paul Iles whose nickname was Hemorrhoids. (Come on, work with me here! Parents can be really thoughtless bastards at times can't they?).

And poor old Gooey!
Helen's mate, Annie, who was also an Infant teacher overheard a Mum shouting to her son.
" Gooey! Gooey, come her!".
Confused she asked," That's an unusual name, how did you come to choose it".
Mum replied," I read a lovely book once!, (That, I doubted very much!), and the hero was called Gooey!".
Thinking there was something strange here, she asked," How do you spell it?".
"G, U, Y !", she replied.

I rest my case. Names are important.

And while I'm on a roll, there are literally hundreds of McCourts in the small Cumbrian town of Whitehaven where I was born. Yet, despite having spent ten years abroad, and living away from that for over thirty years now, I have only met one other person with my surname.

He is my Dentist. Yep, another John McCourt, no relation, or at least I don't think so.

For the past two hundred years, all we've done, as far as I'm aware, is dig coal.

I have always believed that our branch of the family settled in England generations ago to work the pits of West Cumberland, I suppose the same way that other McCourts traveled to other parts of the world to survive potato famines, or other such disasters. In honesty, as far as the family tree is concerned, it's one of those things that I've never actually bothered to look into. It's something I expected to get around to doing sometime in the future. Funny how it seems a little more important now.

I have of course, read Frank McCourt's excellent book , " Angela's Ashes ", and loosely wondered if we were related, him being a teacher like me, and having a resemblance to some of the family. But there the similarities end, and although I started life as the bastard son of a Venezuelan Naval Officer, and had a relatively impoverished upbringing, I knew nothing of the poverty that this man had growing up in the slums of Dublin.

I was born at a better time in history.

I'm Billy McCourt, no relation.

I like the idea of being Billy McCourt, the author, and at this moment in time, to me at least, what I've got to write is important, *and perhaps to someone else, who gets given some startling news, which straight away, in one fell swoop, at the blink of an eye, makes the world you live in a little scarier place, and for me right now that's a good enough reason! I'm waffling a bit, probably because I'm a bit shaky at the moment, did I mention I've got Cancer.*

I'd quite like to be a successful author like Jeffrey Archer, hope I've spelt it right, because there are two of them out there, and what a great idea the other bloke had, writing a book with the same name as somebody famous…I wish I was called P K Rowling, or Edna Blyton, I'd sell millions before somebody found out.

I mean the one with oooodles of cash, a charming and cavalier disposition, an expensive flat overlooking the Thames, and a penchant for prison food.
I could do with a change of image.

I'm a fifty two year old, overweight teacher, and buy all my clothes from cheap shops like Matalan, *but, I usually prefer to wear Lycra.*

I wear Lycra around the house, in town, in restaurants, *at weddings*, and have had to put up with sad looks and comments from all of my kids like." DAD, YOUR NOT WEARING *YOUR TRACKSTERS* TO MY PARENTS EVENING ...PUT SOME JEANS ON").

I'm at an age where being comfortable is so very important.

I'm also a bit scared at the moment, because I've had some not too good news to deal with all of a sudden, and the question of my possible demise has been raised once again, and this little exercise of silently ranting at a computer screen, may or may not help me to deal with what are lots of strange emotions that I'm reluctantly experiencing at this moment.

It could be it's time to tell the world how lucky I've been in life.

One amazing wife, three brilliantly funny kids of my own, great mates, and hundreds of other kids, (but not in any biological sense,) who have enriched my life to date, and that despite one or two of life's little obstacles, like the childhood Asthma, the heart attack at forty, or the failed attempts to become a millionaire without buying a ticket or appearing on a game show, life's been pretty good.

*Or maybe it's because you've just been told I've got Cancer.
And boy, this is something that really puts the wind up you,
especially since your good mate Doren died of it a few years
ago and you still miss her, and that in three or four weeks
time, a really nice bloke you've never met until yesterday is
going to remove a substantial part of your body to get rid of
the bit of slop your pelvis has turned into, the bit that holds
your legs on, and rebuilds you in titanium, and so yes, maybe
it's time.*

But I mean, it's not a bad idea is it? (The book I mean, not the
Cancer bit.)

I got the idea to write mine yesterday, Tuesday 26th June 2007.

It was the day after we had those huge floods in South
Yorkshire, the wettest day in England in fifty years, or so it
said on the news. I remember thinking straight away that my
bit of news today was a hell of a lot more important than
somebody's flooded basement, but like I said, I was still a bit
raw and a still a bit dazed and immediately I felt ashamed, the
poor buggers.
.
When I got home, I "googled, " how to write a book", on the
internet, and the first website that came up was called, "How
to write a book ". Now how's that for coincidence?

Unfortunately, it didn't say " how to write a GOOD book ",
hence the inane ramblings, but then I thought if good old
Barbara Cartland could knock them out in such prolific
quantities, then why not me? (I could call myself Barbara
Bartland couldn't I?)

*And I've given myself a full three to four weeks to get it done,
because that how long I've got before I go under the knife!*

Well, at least the first part. With a bit of luck, it should keep me busy.

Driving home from Birmingham, after receiving the good news, we called in on Laura, the eldest offspring who lives in Manchester, to let her know the news. (At Eighteen years of age, she spent seven months in an orphanage in Brazil, looking after street kids, living mostly on beans and rice. Kids who were abused, sodomized, and kids who were victims of child prostitution. Quite simply, she inspires me.)

She said to be positive. She also said we're all in this together. I hadn't realized this bit, because I was just thinking about myself, and it's a bit of a shock to realize *this isn't just about me at all, it's about all the people who care about me as well. My family, and to a lesser extent, my friends, are involved in this, with me, whether I like it or not, and at this very moment I'm feeling just a little bit of a selfish, and maybe just a little bit humble. So, moving on quickly...*

I've also been told to lose weight....I'm not happy.

The one hundred and four point four kilograms starting weight they mentioned sounded ok to me, only because I didn't know how much that was in real money.

I found out. I'm 16 stones and 3 pounds. (Another bugger moment...bugger!)

I've also been told I need to learn to use a pair of crutches.

I found this bit surreal. Immediately after I was told about the operation, I was introduced to my new friend, Claire the physiotherapist, and given a lesson on, "how to use a pair of crutches". She measured me up, told me what to do, and off I

22

went crutching round the ward, a bit red faced, because there wasn't a thing wrong with me.

Funnily enough, while I was practicing, another physiotherapist appeared out of nowhere, and started walking backwards in front of me, facing me for support, (my support, not hers). She'd obviously confused me for someone who needed help.

So, I thought, "Why not?".
I did three or four, "move the crutches, bad leg, good leg through" drills, as I'd been shown, putting lots of concentration in it, with the new physiotherapist moving slowly backwards, arms all ready just in case I fell.
(Not a wise move, I thought, because if I fell on her, I would crush the life out of her, sort of like throwing yourself under a piano.)
Anyhow, once I had her full attention, I did a few wobbly steps, which wasn't that difficult seeing as I had become a sixteen stone Bambi, I straightened up and moved sort of Bruce Forsyth like into a Strictly Come Dancing dance routine. Well, I was impressed…and the look on her face was priceless. It sort of cheered me up.

Which smoothly, or not, sort of brings me to fruit of my loins number two, our Claire, who always cheers me up.

Claire brings light into my life, an Advertising Representative, former 18 to 30's rep, and until recently, Ann Summers top Vibrator specialist in Yorkshire, where, or so I believe, she has given the women of North Yorkshire, more pleasure than I could ever dreamed of. She has the gift of lighting up the room the minute she walks in. Mind you, the room is usually the kitchen, and is quickly followed by her lighting up the fridge.

Quite simply, everybody loves Claire, and nobody more than me!

Incidentally, I mentioned that I needed to lose weight, and straight away her reply was a text message.
"Dad, it's me Claire, I'm down at the Gym, and it's just got a new machine. I used it for half an hour and it's been making me sick. It's good though, it's got Mars Bars, Kit Kats, Mini Cheddars "...... I've got this sinking feeling that this isn't going to be easy!

But I really don't feel like I've got Cancer.

While I've mooched around the house, waiting to hear this news, I've had to put up with seeing kids from school all over the village, or round our local town, constantly asking, "You don't look sick sir, that's a nice wetsuit. When are you teaching us again? " and "Sir, when are you coming back, we really hate that new supply teacher, he makes us learn stuff"

I should point out that over the years, I've taught some really nice kids and I'm sure my life has had a constant source of richness from many of the amazingly colourful characters I've had in the classroom. (Including some real numbskulls, like," Sir, did you know that if you hit a £2 coin with a hammer, the middle falls out ?..... I've also had the misfortune of teaching some bloody awful kids, kids you couldn't like in a million years, and can see a mile off which of the little cherubs, and when I say little cherubs, I really mean little bastards, who are destined to be regular guests of Her Majesty from a very early age.
"Hiya sir!, how are you doing " shouted Brendan, an ex-pupil, as we bumped into each other in the pub toilet, me there for the obvious reason, and him selling his dope!

My highs have been as high as anyone's, but the lows, well, some of them I could have done without, so I'm taking this opportunity to add a bit about me, and some of the people who have given my journey so far a richness that's made it special. But hey, without life's experiences, we wouldn't be who we are today, we play the cards we're dealt with right, and what doesn't kill us makes us strong! Right? No-one in their right mind, actually believes this stuff, do they?

God I hate these clichés.

All the time I'm typing this, *I'm not having to think about the Cancer*...and that's not bad in itself, because I've managed to avoid saying the word Cancer very much at all, which probably says a lot about how scared I am at this moment.. Cancer, Cancer, Cancer...sorry, just getting used to saying it.

I'm hoping that once the news settles in, I'll be fine, but today, the world is a very different place than it was yesterday...so here goes.

About being Positive.

Everyone says that when you've been diagnosed with Cancer, the most important thing to do is to be positive. Have a positive attitude. Look at all the positives you can take out of it.
But what does being positive mean really?

I need to find out quick!

And with everyone I've met over the last twenty four hours rabbiting on about being positive, Helen my wife, has started acting like she's being positive *and this sort of worries me*. It really does.

Some people are just not the "being positive kind", and we all know who they are! They're the, "the glass is always half empty, never half full," the"what if this happens?", and "what if that happens? " kind of folk. What I really mean to say is that they're the whining buggers who we usually try to avoid, because, *don't they just pull you down* .

Which sort of brings me to Helen, my soul mate, who has been looking at half empty glasses for years.

If she got a job working for The Samaritans, she would bring the waiting list down massively, clearing the back log overnight.

Bodies would be flying off buildings and bridges all over the town, *even the people who'd accidentally dialed the wrong number,* because it's just not in her nature to be positive all the time. She always looks for half empty glasses.

Maybe they're not all bad. Someone has to look for the danger signals and keep an eye on all the bad things that could happen, so maybe there's a place for these people in our world after all... What's important right now is that my wonderful little wife is being positive with love and that really does make it ok.

It's also doing my head in.

Anyhow, today, I'm also finding out that a lot of people, are starting to come out of the woodwork to "be positive and supportive" (I am already getting sick of the bionic man jokes). The point is, *it's not easy to deal with.*

I've known some of these people for years, in fact when my oldest mate, who usually starts his sentences by saying,"...and you know what else really pisses me off? ", (I in turn, usually reply "Everything !"), ... *even he's started being positive.*

I'm not daft. I know what it is that they're deep down thinking, and what they're really trying to do, and although it's incredibly nice to know that you have friends who are worrying and thinking about you in a caring way, and are rooting for you, *the way it works best for me is to leave me alone to deal with this stuff, because I'm really the only one who can.* No messing, no fuss. Bugger off and let me get back to normal quick.
But who's to say I'm right? It's still very early days, and maybe, at some future point in time, things might go tits up, and the support of family and friends will be just what's needed to help pull me through.

So, right at this moment, I'm sort of adrift, but hopefully, things will get easier with time.

<u>Day Two.   Wednesday 27 th June 2007.</u>

The day after the good news and back home.

The main headline today on the BBC news was that we had a new Prime Minister. It showed Gordon Brown was moving house, next door actually. So why he needs a removal van is beyond me. Why can't he get his mates round with a few boxes and walk the stuff in is beyond me. It's only next door for goodness sake!

Oh yes, and Tony Blair was leaving the Labour Party.

Anyhow, *the really important news* of the day was that the flood waters round Sheffield were starting to go down and that makes me feel a bit better, especially as most of the damage is in and around the old mining areas of South Yorkshire, and good people like these have had enough turmoil over the last few years.

I woke up this morning in a better frame of mind, and my sleep seems to have used the time well to deal with yesterdays confusion..

My back is a bit stiff today, possibly from spending most of yesterday on the computer, but it was easier to do this *and keep the world out*, than answer the phone, which seems to be ringing constantly, now that the news of the Cancer and upcoming operation has leaked out.
It was a bit unfair on Helen I suppose, fielding most of the incoming calls, but I really didn't want to talk to anyone much yesterday. The main exception was of course our Laura, eldest daughter, and a very smart cookie. I mean, here I am, trying to keep everything about the operation low key and telling everyone that there's nothing to worry about forgetting that the

eldest one knows something about medical research and knows more about tumors and prosthetics and the like than I ever will.

It's also awkward, because, it seems like a big change has happened already. It's as if all the conversations you have, from now, to the dreaded day, must be positive, (oh yes, that word again,) and real life isn't like that, and it's not been usual for me and our Laura to talk on the phone more than once or twice a week. The once or twice in one day, today, was awkward.

But she is brilliant, determined and tough and I love her, and she is cheering me up.

Speaking of which, yesterday wasn't all doom and gloom because I went to see a "horse whisperer". His name was David and he's a healer.
"Are you coming down tonight then? "asks our Jane, Helen's younger sister.
"Coming where? "
"Mum's house, David the Horse Whisperer is coming round tonight and he's really good 'cause he's sorted out mine and our Sarah's neck already.
"I've got Cancer love, not Distemper ", I reply.
"No, honestly, I'm serious, and he also talks to animals and does hypnosis", says Jane.
I think it's worth pointing out if you haven't picked up on it already, that I am and always have been a bit of a cynic and I'd never met Rex Harrison before, so a visit to Dr Doolittle in my present confused state of mind was, well,....what the hell, what was there to lose.

But, more importantly, it got out of the way the first awkward meeting with the family. They're feeling sorry for you, scared

29

for you, embarrassed and frightened at the same time of
saying the wrong thing that might upset you.

"He talks to the animals? "
"Yes talks to the animals. "

God, IT IS DR DOOLITTLE, and it isn't as if the day hasn't
been surreal enough already, what with the recent news, and
the fact that now I'm starting a new career as an author. Now
I'm off to meet a man who talks to animals.

We actually had a lovely night, probably the most fun I've had
sober and wearing clothes. Everyone took the evening very
seriously, because hey, why not? There wasn't anything to
lose.
Dave put his hand on peoples damaged bits, which in my case
was mainly in the buttocks area, and I should point out that the
last bloke who put his hand on my bum was seriously
threatened with hospital food, but whoa and alas, (whoa and
alas…horse whisperer, get it?), not me. He didn't do a lot for
me this time, in more ways than one. I thought that if I'd been
diagnosed with testicular cancer like Lance Armstrong, there
wasn't a cat in hells chance I'd be here tonight.

Amazingly though, overall, Dave had a positive result, with
aches and pains disappearing from a few people, so it wasn't a
complete waste of time.

Anyhow, that was how yesterday turned out, so here's
something about me, and where I'm coming from, because all
of a sudden, the future has an uncertain look about it, and it's
time to look back and take stock.

Who am I really? And what are the things that have happened
in my life to shape me into who I am today..

I'm in a reflective mood. Today that feels important

So here goes.

I was born into a mining family, in 1955 in Lowther Castle, Whitehaven, which I sometimes forgot to mention was the old Whitehaven Hospital because it sounded more impressive when chatting up girls. It's a coastal town in what is now Cumbria, and on the edge of the most beautiful area of England, the Lake District.

I'd always thought of Whitehaven as an insignificant little town when growing up, the only thing it was famous for was that it was the location of the last recorded invasion of England, way back in the 1600s. In school, it was seen as educationally important to drum the local history into us, and we were forever being told that around the time of the American War of Independence, a certain John Paul Jones, who later went on to become the founder of the American Navy, sneaked into the harbour to set fire to our ships. We were told the story of how the brave and true men of Whitehaven discovered this, and bravely sent him packing.

I now understand there is another version of the facts, a more historically correct version. It seems that on his way to burning our ships, his lads got a little thirsty, stopped off at a local pub and got drunk. One of his lads, would had been here before, apparently took a shine to the place, and let the locals know what was happening, who then kicked JPJ out of town. He then went over the Solway to Scotland to kidnap some local dignitary who wasn't home. It looks like the Founder of the American Navy didn't get a lot right in the early days, starting off the American tradition of buggering things up where invasions are concerned. No doubt if he's been around today, he'd be responsible for Iraq.

But it was real history. Mining wasn't!

It was the here and now, and the pit was where the men in the family worked, While I was growing up, anything to do with the mines which at one time had peppered the Town, couldn't be classed as History. History was about Romans and such like. Mining for me was day to day living, as I've said, the here and now, and the thought that somewhere way back, we as a family, had roots in the history of the town, never entered my head. What is now Haig Mining Museum was then a working pit where Dad worked, Uncle Vic worked, and just before its' closure in the 1980's, cousin Ian worked there as well.

History was something else. And we weren't the kind of family that wasted time looking backward.

I was born the bastard son of a Venezuelan Naval Officer. Sometime in 1954, while working as a nurse in Barrow-in-Furness, my mother had a relationship with my Father who had been in England at the time, commissioning a new ship for the Venezuelan Navy. The result of the relationship was me, born not long after my father returned to his pregnant wife back home. Such is the way of life. I suppose I could have used the more socially acceptable term "illegitimate son of...", but I'm in that sort of mood, and there's a point to make.

My Grandfather was the head of the family, at least he was when my Nan let him, and I grew up in his house until I was ten, with my Granddad, Nana, Mother, and little sister Beverley. He was as hard as nails to anyone outside the family, but that's not how I remember him. I only remember the love he showed for me while I was growing up. Anyway, I remember my Grandfather's small council house as a happy place, with a big coal fire in the front room, which we all sat round, Dad getting the best chair, nearest the hearth. I'd sit on his shoulders and pick out all his grey hairs, and only stopped doing this when I got too big and hurt his shoulders. It was either that or the grey hairs had started to outnumber the black ones, I'm not sure now. He used to take me to watch our local rugby league team where I used to play behind the banking because I didn't have the patience or maturity to watch the game. As far as I was concerned, he was my dad, and I still miss him today. I remember someone telling me a story about him, not long after we'd cremated him.

"By lad, we were all terrified of Jack McCourt when we were growing up. He had a look in his eye which really put fear into you", he stated, confirming the hard man he was, and the soft and warm man he became.

I called him Dad, and I still remember him as the softest, kindest, man I've ever met. Sorry to disappoint everyone, but there were no ten kids in a single bed, shoeboxes in the middle of the road, or bits sold off for body parts, as in Frank McCourt's book. Or was that Monty Python? But Dad did sleep in the single room because of his snoring, and we shared the other two rooms.

I have some really good memories of growing up..
I remember all my summer holidays consisted of walking to Uncle Vic's house, about a mile away, *for the whole six weeks of the summer holiday*, to stay with cousins, Janet and Ian, in their council house down the road. Money was always tight and we couldn't afford proper holidays. I really envied the other kids at school who'd come back from exotic places like Blackpool or better still, Butlins. The furthest I had ever been on holiday was to Nethertown, a village by the sea, six miles away, in a two berth caravan costing six pounds for the whole week. *I remember we had a brilliant week. We could run on the beach, and not have to get a bus or walk home at tea time, it was bliss. I've always thought that really making it in life*

meant being able to stay on the beach and not have to catch a bus home at tea time.

Now, straight off, let me make it clear now that we all lived in council houses in our area, and it was fairly uncommon to know of anyone who actually owned their own house. Even when I went to Grammar School, the vast majority of my schoolmates lived on estates like ours and there was absolutely no stigma whatsoever attached to living in a council house. To be clear here, our estate wasn't like the big inner city sprawls, miles and miles of concrete. It was small, and surrounded by green fields. We lived within walking distance of areas of real beauty, with views from cliff top walks over the Solway where we could easily see the Isle of Man and the south coast of Scotland. I'd often watch the fishing boats head for home before the tide turned and the sunsets along this coastline were simply amazing. To the east of where we lived were the Lakeland hills, only a bus ride away, and I later realized that I'd been fortunate to have had a childhood in such a place. I could escape when I needed to.

It's only later in life and having left the town that I appreciated the good points of the place. There was a strong sense of community on these estates, and the people were generally proud of their hospitality. I miss this today.

We knew how to enjoy ourselves without much money! We learnt to get on with life, and not complain. Mining people were generally proud people who lived a hard life, but maintained very solid values.

Yes, looking back, Whitehaven was a good place to come from.

As a little boy, I was football daft, but realized at an early age I had no talent whatsoever. I had one good foot, and I was useless, but it didn't stop me from playing. I would come in from school in the dreaded dinner van, get into my football kit

34

or old togs, and spend hours playing with Eric Nicholson and Kevin Hodgson on Kells Miners Welfare, where it was football, rugby or cricket for hours at a time, and yes, it has to be said, I'm sure we had better weather then, with long sunny nights, and lots of mates to play with.

I hated being dragged in from the Welfare, where we'd spend hours playing soccer, or cricket, for bed, or any time, but especially at teatime on a Sunday when it was time to get scrubbed and dragged off to church to sing in the choir with Dad. I was often wearing the angelic choirboy stuff with the dirtiest, muddiest knees imaginable because there often wasn't the time to get cleaned up in the kitchen sink.

To get out of it, I often tried to hide when Grandad would come looking for me, so I could keep playing with my mates, but looking back, going to church with my Grandad was, and still, is one of my fondest memories.

Mind you, I was a lot happier when a little later I went to sing in another church choir where choirboys got paid appearance money, and were taken on trips. This in a roundabout way, led to my first experience of climbing a mountain, and developed into a love of the outdoors which just got stronger with age.

So, if I could play football and climb mountains, why did I need to go to school in the school van?

I remember the embarrassment of having to be taken back and forward to school in the school van, yes, the dinner van, (fortunately, there were no dinners in it at the time), because I had Asthma.

Not cool.

And then it used to come back again, at dinnertimes, with the horrible school dinners, (at least mine were free, which was another stigma), and all because I wasn't allowed to walk up the hill from school, because of the Asthma, brought on by the smoke and fumes from the bloody Chemical factory, a few streets away.

Because of the Asthma, I wasn't allowed to play football in the school team, and had to stay in school and do arty things while the rest of the kids had games and God I really hated Art at School, *all because of the bloody Asthma.*

It's funny though, how it all cleared up when we moved to another council house less than a mile away from the shitty Chemical factory, and it all went away. But was it really Asthma? Being ill on the Social Security had it's perks I suppose, clothing allowances and stuff, but it also meant I never got to play for the school team. And with all that talent…yeah right!

I was happy as a small boy, These were happy times.

But sometimes I felt different to other kids, and deep down thought that something was missing. It took about forty years for that Jigsaw to come together.

In fairness I was told about my real father frequently as a small boy, but he was too far away to be real. The idea that I had a real dad who was an officer in the Navy, and from another country seemed exciting and I suppose adventurous, but I couldn't understand it when people thought I was sometimes making up stories, and after a while, I wasn't sure myself what was real, and what was embellished.(So when I first met him at the age of 40, (me that is), a bit slow with age, (him that is), but more from the couple of brain tumors he'd had removed in the 1960's, the whole experience of meeting long lost dad was honestly, a little bit flat, especially when heading back to his house, in the car from the airport to Caracas, he asked me who my mother was! My new brothers and sisters and the way things turned out after meeting them, are a whole different story.

Another thing I suppose was that being illegitimate in a small community in the 1950's was a bit different to being "born out of wedlock" nowadays. Not with the kids you played with, but with the way some narrow minded adults looked at you. Having kids out of wedlock is no longer the social stigma it was and rightly so. Kids don't ask to be born, and I genuinely do remember being looked down upon by some of the grown ups when someone mentioned, "he's Pauline's lad ". In those days, especially in a small community, it was very different. Pauline, my mother wasn't allowed out of the house for the duration of the pregnancy, it just wasn't done, and it sort of scarred her for the rest of her life. I don't think she ever got over the shame of firstly having me, and then, in relatively short space of time, having a divorce from Beverley's father. There were occasions when her pent up frustrations erupted, like the time when my mother lost it in a big way, which she often did when we were kids, and spent a good hour calling me "the bastard ", and, "you're a bastard, you know that? " and a few more choice comments.

 I suppose what made this little bit of drama more memorable than others was that it wasn't that long ago. *I was thirty-nine at the time, and my wife, my kids and my friends were watching the whole thing.*

Looking back, I realize my mother did have a hard life. She had married a scumbag from Glasgow who left her after only a few months, and was left to drag us up. She often behaved like this, behind closed doors, but never when my grandfather was about. But granddad got older, and things changed, not for the better.

From the age of ten, when Dad retired from the pit, life went pretty much downhill. My mother never held a job down for long, and eventually developed mental problems which meant her taking a lot of medications. One Christmas day when I'd be about thirteen, whilst waiting for her useless boyfriend Len to come back from the pub so we could eat our Xmas dinner, she became very very stressed, and lost the plot, and began to threaten my sister with a poker, and not for the first time. Bev was screaming and jumping up and down on the table, (fortunately, dinner was still in the kitchen, so there was no gravy being slopped about all over the place), and the point was eventually reached when I couldn't handle it any more, so I slapped her round the face and took the pair of us off to Uncle Vic's for sanctuary.

We were scared of her as kids.

Sometimes, she'd be shipped of to the Psychiatric Ward in the local hospital, "to have a rest", and I always remember these rest periods as good times. I stayed at my Uncle Vic's and Auntie Marion's house, these being the other really important people in my life where I had regular meals, no coal to carry, and it meant going to school in trousers that had just been ironed, a big bonus in the chatting up girls at school part of life.

By now, we'd moved to a council house of our own, where we lived on what the Social Security dished out and got by, with a little help from Grandad. I suppose this last ranting episode of hers sort of confirmed what I'd known since being a child. Her life had been a difficult one, and we were inwardly resented for ruining her life. She was without doubt, a disturbed woman at the time, who needed help, help, from the medical experts at the time, being to throw drugs in the form of tranquillizers at the problem, which I'm sure was in some way was accountable for many of her emotional outbursts. But then, as kids, maybe we could have done with a little more help and support.
Well, for the record, none of this was our fault.
When I mentioned the cliff top walk over to the lighthouse at St Bees head, it reminded me of the first time I saw a dead

body, that of my next door neighbour and friend, little John Telford who was killed looking for bird's eggs at eleven years old.

We'd been playing in the garden and John, who always had a twinkle in his eye, and a few other lads, decided to go over to Fleswick bay for seagull's eggs. I was going with them because it was more important not to be seen as a sissy than get into trouble with the mums and dads, despite the number of warnings I'd had not to play on the cliffs and how dangerous it was. I was eight years old after all!

We were sneaking out the back way when I heard my Nan shout, "Oi! Get yourself back in here lad!", or words to that effect, and I turned round and sheepishly came back. Deep down, I was relieved.

It was the last time I saw John alive.

His body was found on the rocks below in Fleswick Bay, by his Uncle Sandy, in the early hours of the following morning, and the street went into mourning. His little brother David, who would be about six at the time, pulled me into the house a few days later to have a look at John resting in his coffin upstairs, and I remember it feeling all so normal, and thinking that it could just so easily have been me. A couple of years later, it was Pat McAlone's turn, at just thirteen, and I remember the morning his coffin was brought him out of the house for his final journey. It seemed to be a world where kids took more chances than nowadays, often with the worst possible results.

I never saw another dead body until it was my Grandads' turn to go, and I had a real shock. I flew back from South Africa, and later that night, I visited him at the Chapel of Rest, where I leaned over and I kissed him on his forehead to say my farewell. I was stunned at how cold he was and I quickly realized that what I had kissed wasn't my Grandfather at all, because he'd been a warm and loving sort of person.

What I'd kissed was simply what was left of the packaging.

But I digress. I had more traumas to deal growing up.
At twelve years old, I remember being dumped for the first time. Wendy stood me up, leaving me standing at the Bus Station, all scrubbed up and wearing the new shirt I'd bought with my paper round money. I had clear shiny skin, because my Auntie Marion really did know how to attack a blackhead. There was none of your nambi pambi Clearasil in our house. With a bowlful of hot steam and an hairgrip she soon sorted the buggers out, *and left your head looking like a boil for hours afterwards*. Inside, I all excited, eagerly anticipating all the snogging to come. (Remember when you could snog non stop for twenty eight minutes and just didn't care when your lips went numb, it was how we learned and what we lived for).

She never turned up, and this the week before Christmas.

And no wonder I'm on cholesterol tablets, and had the heart attack. In those days, everybody's food was cooked in a chip pan, and I do mean every meal, unless it was on toast, and that chips and egg were normal at least three times a week. *I didn't know meat had legs*. I just thought all meat came in tins and I genuinely didn't know what a steak tasted like until I was fifteen years old. It was all we knew or could afford at the time, and *beef dripping really was good for you*.

It wasn't all bad. I have some really good memories, especially of my Nana, my best mate Martha!
My Nana, a local character, really did adopted me as her own, and loved me as she did the son she'd lost on his second birthday, many years before. In later years, she could always be found in the Lion, the local pub, afternoon and night with the retired miners. At lunchtimes, she would spend her time betting her pension money on the horses. And did she win? Not very often, and when she did, she kept it very quiet, but it kept her version of sanity intact on a day to day basis.

I've a lot to thank her for. I've since taught Mathematics in school and am very much convinced that the reason that any mathematical talents I may have had, weren't genetic at all, but were rooted in being able to calculate the winnings from horse races, doubles, trebles, four horse accumulators, from the age of about ten. I just thought that Fractions were called Odds.

She once fell down the pub steps, coming out at two O'clock in the morning after a lock in, and broke her collarbone. We had to tell the neighbors she slipped whitening her front steps, a common practice back home. After all, *she was only seventy eight at the time.* I loved her attitude to life.

"Don't eat them pies from Carlisle railway station lad, they're horrible," she once told me, and when I asked her when was the last time she had a pie at Carlisle railway station, she replied, " 1933 !" And this fifty years later!

So as you can gather, we weren't a well traveled lot.

But we were good at Funerals. We didn't have big family parties, and as a child, I don't remember ever going to anyone's wedding. We used to make up for it at Funerals. I still think we have more fun at funerals than many people have at weddings.

After the internment, we'd go back to the house, and it would usually be Martha who, out of the blue, would make a comment, crack a joke, do something which would smash the somber mood wide open, and that was it, out comes the whisky bottle and whatever else, and it was belly laughs for hours on end. It was a gift she had, and I'm sure it went a long way to help with the healing process.
The last funeral I went to in Whitehaven, (actually it was my Nana's and didn't seem all that funny this time), I remember

my Auntie Isobel, Nan's sister telling me that the booze for her funeral is under the bed in the spare room, and it's mounting up nicely. …I can't wait.

Back to today…..

At the moment, Helen's making my Tea, which in itself is strange because she usually can't find the kitchen without GPS and an Ordnance Survey Map. I've spent all day on the computer putting my thoughts down, and it's been a fairly safe place to be today. I think that it's easier to write this book and let others know my feelings by reading about them and me not having to talk about it, I'm not ready to face the world yet. I've sort of ignored everyone, but not in a nasty way. I just need the time to think and let things sink in, without having to deal with the concerns of other people. I'm sure all this fuss will wear off when things have time to settle.

I'm having an early night, keeping my fingers crossed that well meaning visitors stay away.

Day Three Thursday 28th June 2007

Some things never change do they? Today's news was a bit like Deja Vu. Or is it just that it's the same old story every year? I'm not sure.

BBC Breakfast reported this morning that all our British women tennis players have been knocked out of Wimbledon already, where incidentally, it's raining.

Well, what a surprise.

And that the weather forecast for the next few days is also more rain.

What? Wimbledon week?

So I suppose that my prediction, that by the end of the week, all the British men will be knocked out as well will make me something of a prophet will it? And can I say the word prophet nowadays, without having a fatwa taken out against me? I'm not sure anymore…

It's just all so familiar. It's the same at Wimbledon every year is it not?.

I hope it's the same next year!

Funnily enough, today, it's sunny here, in Hunmanby, North Yorkshire, where we live. Our Laura has just been on the phone, and the world all of a sudden seems a brighter place today. I've decided to get showered.

For some reason, yesterday I forgot.

Anyway, yesterday was in the past, and today I've decided that today's the day to get planning properly, sort out how to go about the fight on flab, and build up a bit of top muscle for when I eventually become dependent on the crutches. Of course, today is all about being positive and I've got to spend some time today phoning up the people I ignored yesterday.

Today's the day I become "white lycra man".

Don't get me wrong. First of all I quite like Lycra. I've worn it for years, for walking up and down mountains in, jogging in, cycling in, in fact I've spent a fair chunk of my adult life in Lycra because I find it comfortable. I like wearing it better than designer jeans and trendy tops because, well I just do. I might wear shorts in summer, but lycra does it for me!

But why become "*white* lycra man"?

It's all down to Helen's mate Claire (who, by the way, is drop dead gorgeous, a bit like a Tinkerbell on the dance floor, don't ask, it's a Peter Pan thing),but she's also something of a nutter .

She's into this new fad of "life coaching", and she honestly believes that by imagining me in white lycra, but not in a pervy way, sort of like a Power Ranger, fighting the cancer with a big sword or suchlike, her positive vibes will wing their way across the ether, and give me added strength to fight the foe, or something along those lines. Now, I'd rather spend the time a little differently and imagine her in white silk stockings, but enough said. Also, she's just given Helen a book entitled, " I beat my Cancer ", because, no, she hasn't beat Cancer, and no, she's never had Cancer, but her partner's dad did, and in her own sweet way, she's helping in a real way because she's been there, *and yes, she's being positive.*

The Power Ranger bit sort of brings me onto offspring number three, *The Boy*.

He will always be *The Boy* to me even though I stopped wrestling with him when he was about fourteen, because it hurt too much. He is fairly short and stocky in build, with lovely wavy ginger hair, and has the kindest sweetest nature imaginable. He's also built like a brick shithouse, and if there was a school or an exam for Power Rangers, or Ninjas, he would have come top, no question about it.

He already has a ninja suit from the days a couple of years ago, when him and his equally barmy mates decided to be ninjas, learning all about martial arts in his mate Jonny's back garden, and then trying to toughen themselves up by sleeping out in the woods all night, without a tent. They actually lasted until about two in the morning when they went home to his mates house because they were cold and miserable, and I can only be thankful some poor old lady wasn't out walking her dog and bumped into this lot dressed all in black, carrying samurai swords and wearing wellys with two toes. Her heart would have stopped.

I'm still waiting to talk to him, as he's working as a diving instructor in Greece, (well has been since last Wednesday, not bad for a 19 year old), and I'm missing him already, but I'm thinking that like a lot of tough looking men, inside them is very often a soft, sensitive core, often well hidden, and part of me thinks I'd rather keep him away from what's happening to me at present, because I think that maybe out of the three of my kids, he'd be the one who'd find things the most difficult.

I also finding out today, that I'm not the only one who's coming to terms with things.

Helen went to work this morning, but was back home by eleven. She just found it too difficult, and came home. She then launched into a tirade, and said that I'm not allowed to go anywhere out of her life, because she can't work the television buttons, and thinking about it, who's going to change the clocks, when they move forwards and backwards each year. I'm surprised she knows that the clocks get changed at all, because they're usually done by the time she gets out of bed, mind you, I usually change the one in her car about three weeks after the event because she's turned up late or early for something or other.

So, the theme for today is being positive.

Breakfast this morning was porridge made with skimmed milk, with added honey and blueberries because according to "her who thinks she should be obeyed", blueberries are "superfoods".

Bloody nonsense, Steak and Chips area superfoods.

Another thing! She keeps throwing these mini-yoghurt things at me, because she says they'll boost my immune system. Our Laura reckons one of her Scientist mates has done a study on this stuff and she reckons it's all a load of hogwash and so we're looking for another Scientist mate who might have done the English Fry-Up Study, and has results to say pork sausages are a super food, but maybe I'm grasping at straws.

I suppose the other bit of good news is that according to our scales, I'm down to sixteen stone, three pounds off, none of the metric nonsense, the same weight Frank Bruno was when he fought Mike Tyson. Unfortunately, I'm a foot shorter at five feet ten, and let's be honest, three pounds in two days? Maybe it's time to check the scales. ....Another bugger moment...bugger!

So, how did David the Horse Whisperer really do? It's the day after being touched up, and I definitely don't feel any different. Sarah rang up earlier, and said he would like to have another go and continue with the treatment, but I'm thinking I may give it a miss. However, Helen does feel better, and so does our Claire. Not amazingly so, but a definite improvement.

Poor old Tim, Helen's brother got worse.

So, something new I want to think about.
Is there anything in the spiritual approach to all this? Like prayer and that sort of stuff.
Or is the whole business of miracles just a state of mind thing? There used to be a bloke two thousand years ago who could do David's thing wasn't there?

But then, I've heard or read somewhere that Cancer can be caused by a state of mind. and that sometimes stress, perhaps caused by having an unhappy job, or caused by miserable lifestyle, maybe living in a manner which sort of contradicts what you are all about, all of this can cause a constant state of frustration in a person, which may then produce toxins that can build up in the body, and then cause Cancer.

Now if that isn't in the mind, then what is?

Maybe I shouldn't be so cynical and dismiss David's "Gift" out of hand, but instead try to embrace the positive nature of what he does, which, I suppose, is similar perhaps to what prayer does for those that believe.

I'm not sure, still a bit unclear and wobbly, but like I said, it's very early days, and I'm still feeling my way.

By the way, have you noticed the number of times I've used the word Cancer. I'm settling down nicely.

Oh yes, and the flowers….People keep sending flowers, to cheer me up, but am I right in thinking we equate flowers with funerals?

It's a bit miserable don't you think?

I mean it's all well and good right now, having the house full of lovely flowers, with beautiful colors and lovely sweet fragrances, but what about two weeks from now, when they'll all have died and decomposed, and there's bits of dead petals all over the carpet. Somebody, probably me, will have the job of putting them in the dustbin. Thoughtless I say, damn thoughtless.

Now silk flowers I can understand.
What's that?

They're probably not for me anyhow?

I never thought of that.

….and another thing, we're just not good with flowers.

I mean we like a nice garden like everyone else, but we don't like gardening. Every year Helen buys the bedding plants in little plastic trays at Easter. And every year, around about September, I put the same trays, usually with the plants still in them, into the recycle bin. (Really, they go straight into the dustbin but I'm not telling her that.)

In honesty, I've really been touched by people's kindness, cards coming through the letterbox from friends and family. I've been cheerful enough, so here are some more memories.

So here goes, like most young men, I hated my teenage years.

Well, not entirely true, because I had my good moments and very much enjoyed life when I reached nineteen years old. Up until then, I was spotty faced, despite Auntie Marion's regular attacks with the hairgrip, greasy haired, usually skint, and was, like many teenage boys, very, sexually frustrated. The Latino genes had kicked in, in a big, big way, and despite the bravado, I really didn't have much of a clue about girls....some things never change do they.

And it didn't help much when my mother kept selling my bikes.

Grandad taught me to ride a bike. I loved cycling, still do, and as a kid, we just couldn't afford one. Dad had just retired from the pit, and money was tight.

Neil Tolson, a kid in my class got a new racer, and his mam (not mum, because we didn't have mums, we had mams, because to us Whitehaven lads, mums were something soft kids had), gave me his old bike, and although it was old, and nothing special, you can't imagine the freedom it gave me. Mind you, in return I gave Neil my collection of football programs and bet they're worth a fortune now.

I went everywhere I could on my old bike. *I had my freedom, and that was enough.*
But, it was an old bike, and when it broke down for the last time, I was heart broken.
Luckily, the other really important man in my life, my Uncle Vic, saw how devastated I was, went straight into town, and bought me a second hand racer.

It cost him ten pounds, which was a lot of money in those days, but it meant I could travel even further, discover more, and it was brilliant.

In fact the day after he bought it, Vic remembers coming home at six a.m., on his motorbike, after a night shift at the pit, and seeing me riding up and down the road on it, with a big smile on my face. .

I would finish my paper round, or milk round, whichever I had at the time, get on my bike, and ride.

I hated delivering papers. I remember my paper round being nearly three miles long, and the paper bag the old witch in the paper shop gave me had a worn strap which dug into my shoulder and really hurt, until I'd delivered enough papers to make the bag lighter, and when I complained and asked for a new one, refused to change it.

So, with my £1 a week wages, off I went exploring because I could ride off into the Lake District, and go on serious expeditions, sometimes doing fifty or sixty miles, and life was good. Well, I was only about eleven or twelve.

And then my mother sold my bike.

I came in from school one day and it was gone. For her to sell my bike, knowing how much I loved it, I knew then that times were hard. To help out, I used to carry coal on an old rusty bike with metal rims from Dad's house or Uncle Vic's house, because they got subsidized coal from the pit. We didn't, and couldn't afford it, and it was a job that had to be done, by me, as the only man in the house, because there was no gas central heating in those days, and coal was our only source of heating. But nevertheless, it was a job I hated, and I did my best do it in the dark, to make sure I wouldn't be seen by any of my mates, or much worse still, by girls.

I eventually got another bike, using my paper round money as a deposit, but I had to pay for it myself. My mother had finally agreed to buy it on hire purchase, providing I paid the money off each week at what was then, seventy five pence.

We had to sign for it in my mother's name because for some unknown reason, my name was already credit blacklisted, apparently by Kay's catalogue, at the tender age of twelve, for non payment….. now I wonder why?

Still, I couldn't figure out why, after about nine or so months, I was still paying off my bike. I then caught my mother paying it off one Saturday morning and giving the man who came collecting, a mere *thirty five pence*. Don't forget, this was in old money, pre-decimalization so to speak, and I quickly realized she'd been keeping back some of my bike money, and putting it into the kitty.

Imagine how miserable I felt to know I'd be paying my bike off until I was seventy, but I suppose, looking back now, times were tougher than I ever realized.
Not as miserable though, when a few weeks later, I came home from school again, and bugger me, *she'd sold my bike again.*

Today, at the impressionable age of fifty two, I own three really good bikes, top quality bikes, and sort of treasure them.

Salvation, in those difficult years, also came in the form of a 6ft 11" tall youth club leader called Brian Harris, the youth leader at the Y.W.C.A.

Yes, you can read, the Young Women's Christian .Association.

The Y.W.C.A. had a mixed youth club and was the place where I first learned to snog, especially with Mandy Gordon, at Saturday night discos, great because the red light bulbs hid my big red boil of a head after another Auntie Marion visit.

I must explain Mandy was my first girlfriend, no, sorry, I was her first boyfriend, that's right, and it wasn't her who dumped me at the Bus Station.
I think she dumped me outside of the Y.W.C.A.

Brian Harris introduced me and a few other mates to Fell Walking and Youth Hostelling, with trips to Scotland but more memorably Wales, and I owe this man a great deal.
I believe that much of the man I am today, and I hope that's a good thing, is down to the influence of Brian Harris, a brilliant role model, and I have tried on a number of occasions to catch up with him simply to say thank you, but have failed miserably.

And while I'm in a whinging mood, here's something else.

I really hated school as well.

I suppose I was lucky enough to leave Whitehaven Grammar School with a few O levels, because they certainly helped a few years later, but my first memory of the school, was the School blazer. It was a Grammer School, but this was the beginning of the Comprehensive School era, and therefore wasn't quite as posh as it sounded. Somebody should have told our pompous little shit of a Headmaster though, because I'm sure he thought it was Eton School who had acquired his services, the way he used to strut about the place.

"Where's your blazer boy?", was all I remember hearing when he spotted me.

My first memory is the school blazer, because we had *three different ones*, depending how much money your family had, and I had always thought school uniforms were designed to make all the kids equal?

There was the expensive blazer from a bespoke tailor in town, a co-op one at about half the price, and the cheap plain one from the Beehive, that your mother stitched lime green braid to.

I started with the Co-op one, but didn't have one after the first year because the grant money had been spent on something else.

I then spent a lot of time hiding from the Headmaster, at least until cousin Janet got a new one, and handed theirs down, and a girls one at that.

Over the years, I had genuinely forgotten how much I hated the place until I went back for a reunion at the age of forty, and what a bloody shambles. The memories just came flooding back, and not a single old teacher had bothered to turn up.

Surely they all hadn't died off.

Small towns, and a selective education system seem to bring out the worst in small people. At the age of forty, McAllister, a kid in my class at school, from the age of five until senior school, *was still the same tosspot he was at school.* He actually ignored me!

I did in fact meet up with Mandy Gordon again, and we had a lovely chat about a number of things, and I think numb lips came into the conversation at some point.

My mainstay at school was running, and by being on the school cross country team, I got to go to away matches all over the County and occasionally,sometimes beyond. We'd get on the coach early Saturday morning from the bus station to visit other schools for away races, and on the way home, it was a scramble for the back seat where we usually played three card brag, all the way home. I usually walked home from the Bus Station afterwards because I had lost my bus fare, but I loved these days out and it meant I could see new places, and this was very important to me.

I wasn't talented by any means, but by running cross-country, and in the summer, doing athletics, I got to stay behind after school for training, very often being the last person on the school grounds, and it meant I could have a hot shower every night, and got to go home as late as possible. School after hours was a refuge.

I remember our house as a miserable place, and that almost everything in our house was donated second hand. My Grandad's sister Lizzie had lent my mother ten pounds to buy old suite from a sale, which she was supposed to pay back at a pound a week, and when she didn't, there was often a knock at the door which meant keeping quiet until she went away. We had threadbare carpets, old metal hospital beds, and what looked like grey woolen hospital blankets which had come from a hospital that had just closed down.

Everything was metered. We had a metered television which had a slot for 50p's, as did the electricity meter, and what was heartbreaking was when you put the last 50p into the TV slot, when it was the electricity that had dropped. Luckily this only happened in Summer, and thank god we didn't have a gas meter, because we didn't have gas. It would have been pure confusion.

In winter when it happened, it just went dark, stayed dark, and no more 50p's meant an early night.

I used to get up in the mornings early to a cold house and had to light the fire before venturing out to deliver milk or papers, whichever I was doing at the time, but at least the house was warm when I got back. I laugh now when I remember one particularly cold morning when I stuffed old newspapers inside all my clothes because some mate had told me they made good insulating material, and they kept out the cold. The other lads on the milk van were helpless with laughter because I'd overdone it, looked like the Michelin man, and couldn't bend down to pick up the milk bottles. The best part was walking through the estate before we started with another lad, Jackie, who was a fanatic about astronomy, and, him being older than me, used to tell me all sorts about the stars and stuff that has stayed with me for years. I believe he went on to become very successful later in life, in this field.

No shoeboxes in the middle of the road, but no silver spoons either. I survived, and then I made my first big mistake by joining the Marines.

Back to today….

It's funny, but I've noticed that since people have heard I've got cancer, they find it very difficult to say no to you. Every favour I've asked anyone has met with a resounding, "no problem…". I might start asking for more favours….It's also amazing how everyone agrees with everything you say. It could have advantages……?

Today, I feel great. I haven't left the house, but I've had a shower, got cleaned up, and got going. Writing this is doing me good, taking my mind off things for hours at a time, forcing me to face up to stuff, and look at the number of times I used the word cancer today. But it's all become real today, the shock is wearing off, and I really do know I'm going to be ok. I'm getting into this writing lark. Maybe it's the three F's, friends, flowers and fonecalls, (sorry not a real word, but best I can do), that are doing it, but I do know I'm going to be ok.

The Oracle has spoken.....I told you so, didn't I?

Did I not say yesterday, did I not, that we wouldn't have anybody who could last to the end of the first week of Wimbledon. And now with Tim Henman out, Well, I told you so.

And I've just got this text message:-
"The streets of Rotherham and Sheffield now echo to the cries of "Super, Smashing, Great ", as "Bullseye" speedboat winners finally get the chance to use them!" ....It doesn't take long does it?
English humour. There's nothing like it anywhere else in the world.

And here's some other news from today.

The BBC reported that a bomb has been discovered in London. No. sorry, they didn't actually say that. What they said was, and I quote. *"a potentially viable explosive device* has been found in...... *a what?* Has the world gone daft? It's a bomb for goodness sake. Well two actually. Car bombs. And why is it that in the Second World War, when the Germans dropped lots of bombs on London, they were called bombs, they went bang, it was that simple.

Anyhow, I'm glad they didn't go off.

"A potentially viable explosive device". What a load of bollocks.

In schools, where I've spent some considerable time lately, it would be immediately abbreviated to a PVED, because

Educational "experts", (and I use the word experts very carefully), love four letter acronyms.

We've got CASE, short for Cognitive Acceleration in Science Education, whatever that means.

We've got ASDAN, short for Award Scheme Development and Accreditation Network, sorry, that's five letters, and here I thought it was a Dam in Egypt.

But my all time favorite, spotted in a Bradford school, is Curriculum Related Assessment Profiles. Because that's just what it is. CRAP!

And where does this stuff come from. I'll tell you. It comes from so called "Experts", who couldn't survive in a classroom in a month of Sundays, and managed to escape as quickly as possible.
I'm sure they make all this stuff up to justify their ridiculously high salaries, and then they go and change it all a year later to keep teachers on their toes. And what's more, we've now we've got schools full of power dressed "Managers" who see that this stuff gets done, and thereby justifying their own exorbitantly high salaries.

It's all wrong. It should be about the kids.

And why power dress in a school at all. We've done away with chalk and inkwells, fair enough, but everyone knows that the best teachers were always the scruffiest teachers. They usually were the ones with leather patches on their elbows. That's their Jackets, usually their tweed Jackets, and usually stinking of pipe smoke. Am I right? Of course I am!

Teachers cared about kids then!

It's not really any different in Hospitals is it? They've got more managers than Doctors and Nurses, and that can't be right?

I blame Maggie Thatcher, of course, for all this.

"Let's turn everyone into a manager, because managers are middle class, and middle class people always vote Tory." was the strategy of the Government at the time. And why not let them buy their own council houses while we're at it? They'll all be falling down soon enough.

It nearly worked. Well ok, it did work for a while…

But our Tony isn't daft, is he? He turned the Labour Party into the Tory Party, and outflanked her.

So, for the record, LIST…Life Is Too Short…so, COTC….Cut Out The Crap, and here endeth the party political broadcast for the Common Sense Party.

Strange day today, I had my first spiritual visit.

It had to happen of course, and I'm fairly glad it was Jeff. Jeff's the local Vicar, nice bloke, used to be an electrician. The sort of bloke you can relate to! He's the, "Before I let God into my life, I used to drink, smoke, swear, and watch porn like the other fellers ", sort of chap.
Well, I'm not that bad as an active Non-Christian…… I don't smoke, which sort of reminds me of something else entirely.

The kids told me and Helen, the other week, in front of all our mates at the local pub, that it's my fault for them being traumatized in a, how shall I put it, a minor sexual way, when they were younger.

Through, "Blackbeard's Ghost, apparently.

Someone, but most definitely not me, had somehow, still a mystery to this day, taped one of the Adult Channels, (or maybe it was called the Adult Channel, I'm not sure), and taped it over Andrew's favorite tape, "Blackbeard's Ghost", when the kids were little. (I used to think it was his favorite, because I found it in his bedroom a few years later....)

But why tell us in the pub, in a room full of our mates, and so many years later, and thinking it was me...well that was unfair, grossly unfair.

In my defence, m'lud, I must point out that Helen has never mastered the art of the telebuttons, I mean she still asks "What's on proper TV? "

We've one thousand sky channels but apparently only "four normal TV channels". so a simple slip...

But there are always the positives, I mean, would our Claire have developed the technical awareness she has, of the complete Rampant Rabbits range of Vibrators without such a liberal, educational experience?
I don't actually know what they're called, and apparently they're all very different with different erogenous thingmebobs and other sensitive thingamagigs,

Sorry, back to Jeff and serious again.

The thing about Cancer is that it's associated, in most people's mind, with death.

People get Cancer, and people die, that's it.

Therefore, sometime or other, it's fairly certain that someone from the local church is going to wander round, and make sure that, should the end be nigh, you end up going up to the right place. Also, who are better qualified in the miracle department, should it be required, than the local god squad. I should mention that while I'm not the most God fearing soul, Helen is, and for many years, has been actively involved in Church, and likes the modern, happy, clappy variety. And so are Laurie and Patricia, two of my favorite people of all time, Helen's Uncle and Auntie.

So, it was inevitable.

Being honest, Laurie and Patricia came across earlier this month for a chat, and to offer support, and, as always, it's good to see them. The uncomfortable bit I suppose is towards the end of the conversation when, for the best reasons in the world, Christian people want to pray with you and for you, and the way I see it, it would only be less than respectful to refuse such a well meant request.
So Jeff came round, and we prayed together, or, more accurately, he did, much the same as Laurie and I had done a few weeks ago. I just sat there while Jeff said his stuff, and that was it.
"I'll come round and visit again if that's ok?" said Jeff on his way out.
That's fine by me. Whether it does any good in the long run, only time will tell, but I'm open to anything right now, and I don't mean that in any negative way, because there is a long history of weird and wonderful things that have happened to people who have put their faith in their God. So Jeff, Laurie, and anyone else, bring it on.

I can honestly say that today has started well, and I feel great. I've just had a quick phone call from our Laura to say she was coming over tonight. The weather is lovely, and I might have a wobbly walk on the beach later.

Jane rang again, not about the Horse Whisperer, but a Vet she knows who has developed an all singing and dancing cure of Cancer, well, at least in dogs.
Our Jane is nothing if not passionate, but what's in store tomorrow?

"I know a farmer who can cure Cancer, but it means spending the night in a sheep dip?".
(Remember what I said, open mind and all that, and being positive with love....)

And I finally managed to talk to The Boy. And boy, is he upset, because in his mind, he's doing the Cancer means death thing, and unlike me, who's had a few days to settle down to the news, he's still in shock. And it hurts, it hurts me, because I'm his Dad, and I love him, and there's nothing I can do to take that hurt away.

It's my own fault I suppose. When he went off I'd told him I had a tumour but sort of forgot to mention that a tumour actually means Cancer. Now he wants to come home. His new job, living the dream, everything he's worked towards all year, and it's just disappeared from his mind, because he wants to come home. This is his first big "life sucks" situation, and I can't protect him from it. Did I mention I have three fantastic kids?
So, we've all talked to him, settled him a little, and we've all made a decision for him to wait three days to calm down, and when we're a little stronger, we'll make a decision. I'll talk to him again tomorrow and see how he is!

What nonsense! Absolute bollocks!

62

He's just like me, and no matter what I say to him, he's stubborn and he'll be on his way home as soon as he can get a flight! I know him!

Helen and I went for a walk on the beach, not far, but enough, held hands, whispered sweet nothings but didn't need to talk much or waste words, no need. The colors seemed really intense today, more than I can remember for a long time.

We should do this more often.

Day Five - Saturday, 30th June 2007.

What can I say? It's raining again. But why be surprised. It's still the first week of Wimbledon, and it always rains.

Why haven't they got a roof on Centre Court?

I suppose it would be a waste of money, seeing as we British never get anyone through to the second week, and at home, we've all lost interest.

It's like the World Cup, when England get knocked out, on penalties.
It's all over…. Nobody cares anymore.

Not a lot of new news today, it's Saturday, just a little bit about a bomb being discovered in Ibiza. *Yippee! The word they actually used was bomb,* and Yippee, by the way, it was a false alarm.

So, it was a little bit of a shock to see Glasgow Airport.

As far as I can tell, two suicide bombers have tried to drive a 4x4 full of petrol and gas canisters into the Airport terminal and from what I can gather, they made the mistake of lighting the blue touch paper while still driving the car. Doh.
Oh yes, and the 4x4 was wider than the door it was supposed to drive through.

There's nothing like Military Planning, and this was nothing like Military Planning…

A witness reckoned one of them was shouting "Allah. Allah, Allah", whilst trying to fight with a policeman, but I reckon he was shouting "Arrgh, Arrgh Arrgh ", because the dozy sod had just set himself on fire.

Is it a coincidence that this is happening just when Gordon Brown has taken over the country? Couldn't they just have sent a letter to the Newspapers like everyone else who's got something to complain about that nobody else is interested in? It is a bit worrying though. Not a great start for Gordon!

So, moving on, it's raining again, but I just don't care. Cue the theme from "Rocky", because sadly, that's just what I've got playing in the background. I love the Rocky films, and his turtles, Cuff and Link, and I'm sitting here in my Lycra cycling shorts, (no Claire, they're not white), having just spent the best part of an hour training.
Not quite running up the Town Hall steps with a bunch of screaming kids chasing you, which wouldn't work for me, because there are only two steps outside our Town Hall, *and the kids I teach today can't run!*

But it's a start.

I've done about 15 minutes on my spinning cycling bike, because I need to build up the old leg muscles, spent about 20 minutes going up and down stairs pretending I only had one leg, 10 minutes grumbling and recovering because it's a hell of a lot harder than it looks, bloody hell, and the rest of the time trying to build up the old arm and chest muscles with our Andrew's dumbbells. I am also enjoying the happy hormones, amazing, but legal tax free drugs, and better that any you can buy in a school toilet. Honest kids.

I also got some get well cards today, which really cheered me up. Eight to be precise. They were from the kids at school, one from my form class, and one each from each of the classes that I teach in school. The comments were great, because kids are funny, but what made me laugh the most was that all eight were in pink envelopes and all three were identical. They also arrived six weeks after one of my classes had actually left and must have been sitting in someone's out tray which sort of confirms my theory about school managers.

Maybe it's the Ofsted "get well card policy", set down for schools to send a get well card to someone to show they are caring people. And schools really do care....

Whatever, they couldn't have cheered me up more if they'd come from Ernie.

The boxes of fruit were lovely though!

We spoke to Andrew today who had got hammered on Jack Daniels last night.

He's feeling much better.

I'm now having to remortgage the house to pay for phone calls to a Greek Mobile, because when I said we, I meant everyone, Me, Helen, Laura, Claire, Carl, Alex, Mother in Law, and Uncle Tom Cobbly and all. Waste of money though, he reckons he'll be home by Tuesday. I'm now thinking that if I survive the next few months, I'll be bankrupt....

We'd gone through lots of scenarios, me voting for going out to Kos to see him,, rather than him coming home to see me, with the added bonus of escaping the awful weather, with the forecast in England for next five days is rain!
Helen is dead against the idea, because of the risk of infections from the mosquitoes, which might put me at risk during the operation.

But amongst all this, a subtle change has occurred in the McCourt household. It's worth mentioning.

We had switched roles lately, the family rallying to look after dad, and dad feeling a bit helpless, but we're slowly getting back to normal, and Dad's getting his old job back. By agreeing to bring Andrew home, I'm putting Helen and the kid's wishes first, and isn't that what a good Dad does.

The big difference today is that I'm good, really good, and for the next few days, it's not about me at all, it's about our Andrew. Claire got it in a nutshell, one sentence, "He needs to come home". So we've spent yet another fortune on phone calls to try and organize his flight, but he reckons he's already got it sorted through his boss.
Laura said, "We need to be together ".

They are close. *They didn't tell us about Blackbeard's Ghost for years!*

Our fault I suppose. For years, all our holidays were spent in an old static caravan in the Lake District. (When it got dismantled a few years ago, we learned it was over forty years old.) No electricity, only gas lights and even an old gas fridge I bought out of the yellow pages. But we loved the caravan, we loved Wasdale, and we still do.
It meant the kids could open the door, disappear together, usually for hours on end, and come back when they were hungry or tired.

They played together.

When it rained, they played board games, card games, made up games, but *they played together.* So they are very close!
The boy is hurting, so were all hurting, and so he's coming home. Great!
So I have declared this a moaning free day!
And Laura and Claire are now good with the Cancer thing. We went to visit our Claire and Carl , her feller, with Laura and

Alex, her feller. (I never know what to call them, boyfriends? partners?, Fellers is safe).
They decided to stay and have a night out in Scarborough together and let me and mum, (yes, were softies and use the word mum), come home on our own. They had a good night together.

And so did we.

That's it for today.

<u>Day Six - Sunday 1ˢᵗ July 2007.</u>

Guess what. I'm seriously considering stopping doing the daily weather report, because it's getting me down. If I just mention the weather when it's nice and sunny outside, it'll save a bit of time and a substantial amount of ink, *and it'll be positive.*

There's also the fact that I'm stiff all over from all the exercise yesterday, that's making it difficult to get started today, but like the song says " When the going get tough, the tough get going, " Yeah right.

Glasgow Airport is opening up again slowly.

The other big news is that it's now illegal to smoke in public places in England. Why has it taken so long to be introduced into England, when the rest of Britain has been smoke free for ages? Does passive smoking cause Cancer? Have they only just found out? Isn't life strange? Isn't life ironic?

I really do like being English because it's the best excuse we have for acting daft. I mean, I once took a group of kids up Scafell Pike and while they were congratulating themselves on conquering England's highest mountain, a bunch of Morris Dancers turned up, put on an old cassette player, and did their thing with the bells and ribbons and stuff, ... and just had the kids were getting over the shock, the fell runners landed. Where else in the world would this happen?

I rest my Case.

Cancer, Cancer, Cancer...see no problems now. In fact I quite like mentioning it now to see the look of fear in people's faces.

Today was a truly grand day.

Did the exercises this morning, a little more than yesterday, and although I'm still finding it hard work, as Magnus Magnussen used to say, "I've started, so I'll finish."
Then we had Sunday dinner.
I love Sunday dinner at home. Helen hates cooking it because it uses up a full day, but loves the atmosphere, and sitting round the table, the five of us and the In-laws, is sort of right. We know Nana, (Helen's mum) is going to tell Claire not to get fat again, not that she ever was, (It's my genes!), because sensitive she isn't, and that sometime during the meal, Eddie, (Helen's dad), is going to mention Viagra.
It's a good time to be together. The first year we were married, I sent Helen home to her mums, *from Germany*, to learn how to make Yorkshire puddings and Gravy, because her mum's were second to none. No doubts, sometime in the future, our kids will say the same wonderful things about their mum's cooking.

We ate the Christmas Turkey that we've had in the freezer since last December, when we all had a family night out, and won the raffle, (well Laura did). It's quite vivid, because the week before we'd won two cases of beer in another raffle (well, Laura did), and I remember thinking that all we need to win next week are the sprouts, and Xmas will be well and truly sorted out.

We all spoke to The Boy on the phone, for ages, and today, he really does feel a bit better, (See, it confirms my theory that getting over an initial shock is a three day thing), and he's coming home for a week only, enough time to see everything is fine, and then off again, to get back to normal as soon as possible.

Sitting down to Sunday dinner, the atmosphere was a little awkward at first. It's obviously the Cancer thing because it's

70

still very early days, but it wasn't long before things returned to normal.

"You surely can't eat another pudding Claire?", chirps up Nana.

"Twice a week, three times on a Sunday, is my secret for keeping young" was the offering from Grandad, still on about his little blue pills, and who surprisingly stayed awake this week.

Later, we spent the night watching Princess Diana's birthday party on the TV. Isn't it amazing that Tom Jones' hair just keeps getting darker and Elton John's hair just keeps getting longer, although why he finished the show dressed like the Penguin from a Batman film beats me.

Another thing worth mentioning...*the good thing about having Cancer is that you don't have to do the washing up!*

<u>Day Seven – Monday 2nd July 2007.</u>

Today, there was no weather, and there was nothing on the news. .
But at this very moment, every smoker in England is wearing wellies, and standing outside in the rain, under an umbrella.

It's been a sort of," nothing happening day", today. Not a good day.

I didn't do any exercise because I felt too stiff from yesterday, but, being honest, I just couldn't be bothered. I got out of bed early this morning, full of good intentions of going to practice round the village with my crutches, a bit of "Outdoor Crutching ", for the first time, and just as I was about to go out the front door, the heavens opened. So I didn't bother!

I could blame Hugh Laurie though.

Don't get me wrong, I love Hugh Laurie. He's a brilliant actor, terrific in Jeeves and Wooster, and I'm a big fan of his latest series, "House", which is superb hospital drama.

But the episode I watched today had a scene in it where someone said something like, and I quote, " …bone pain is the worst kind…", and I felt my blood chill a little.
I mean, I'm not stupid! I know it's only TV, but instantly, this up and coming operation just became a bit more real. I felt vulnerable all of a sudden and so what followed was pretty much a flat day.

I suppose it's just the way the mind works. Tomorrow, I'll wear white lycra, and fight off the demons,, but I'll wear it under my jeans..

It's left me in a sort of somber mood this morning, so here's a bit more about how I became me, to take my mind off the present.

When I left school at sixteen, I joined the Marines, Junior Marine, then Marine 2nd Class, Service Number RM 29*** My rifle number was 2**30. Someone told me I'd never forget these numbers, and they were right.

I thought becoming a Marine would make me a man, but I was wrong. That came much much later.

Looking back, joining the Marines was probably the worst decision I ever made, but it seemed a good idea at the time. The attraction was the outdoor kind of life and I love the outdoors, but I've since learned this only applies to the warmer months of the year. I could easily hibernate the Winter away; it's the latino blood. The other attraction was the three good meals a day and most importantly, *clean, white, cotton sheets.* I have this thing about cotton sheets, even to this day. I'd spent the last five years either sleeping under horse blankets on yellow Bri-Nylon sheets, which at some time, my mother had tried to iron, melted, leaving behind nasty little globules of hard plastic, which scratched my body to bits.

I still have the scars!,

Or maybe it was the two years I'd just spent sleeping in a boy's size sleeping bag when I was nearly six feet tall, after sewing in the grey horse blankets to keep me warm, after I'd halfway sewn up the end you climb in, so that just so my head could stick out, and stopped my shoulders from getting cold.

Joining the Marines got me away from home. And the family went to pieces.

More accurately, our Beverley cracked up.

Not straight away, but I hadn't realized that, in her life, I was more than just her big brother. I was the man about the house and a sort of the calming influence in her life, and leaving her was a bad decision.

I actually enjoyed the little time I was a Marine, all of it in training, and it did give me a confidence that I didn't previously possess.

But real confidence came much later.

I was gutted when I left to go home for compassionate reasons just a few weeks before the end of Commando Training, and even now, so many years later, I still look on the whole thing has unfinished business.

But the lowest point happened during my first Xmas leave. I'd gone back home for Christmas, looking forward to seeing my mates, and had money in my pocket for the first time ever, a whole twenty eight pounds to last the three weeks, a small fortune in those days. But by the time my mother had taken most of my money for my board and lodging, obviously more expensive at Xmas, I was left with less than ten pounds to see me through. It meant that I'd had to do some babysitting....*a Marine babysitting....* to get some extra spending money to see me through the festive period. I was gutted.

My self image at that time plummeted to an all time low.

There I was, desperately trying to be a man, and in the blink of an eye, I was back to pushing the rusty bike up and down the road carrying coal, and babysitting. What was much worse was that while I'd been away, the house had been neglected. It was dirty and uncared for, and had only three light bulbs in the whole place. We constantly had to move them from room to room, although we kept one in the toilet for obvious reasons.

What was much, much worse was that our Beverley was running wild.

My mother had regained her freedom, which I suppose had to happen at some time, when you consider the hardship she'd had bringing us up. She'd got into the habit of spending most of her time up at the useless boyfriend Len's house, and our house was just left to deteriorate.

The house had been totally neglected, and so had my sister..

My worst memory of that non too festive period was that of coming home late one night, to find that the bulb in the toilet had blown. I sat down in the darkness only to find that someone had *shit on the toilet seat*, and yes, you've got it, *I sat right in it*, in total darkness, and *no f...ing toilet paper*.

Merry f...ing Xmas!

I went back to the Marines two days early to a very empty barracks in Deal, Kent, but for me, life had just got better. I was back to sleeping in cotton sheets, and that was just fine, but all I'd done was run away from life's problems.

Back in Whitehaven, Beverley was still running wild!

It all came to a head a couple of months later, when she was admitted to A Ward, after an attempted suicide. This was the Psychiatric Ward at West Cumberland Hospital, where my mother used to go for her "rest periods".

When I got there, she was in a ward, having a fit of hysteria, all the while hiding a long sliver of glass from the hospital staff. She wasn't well, and so, on compassionate grounds, I left the Marines, came home, and eventually got a job at *the same bloody chemical factory that had irritated my Asthma as a kid.*

But hey, I was a Marine and I could handle it.

I'd felt my world had fallen in on me.

Fortunately, I had left school with a GCE in Chemistry, and this had gotten me a job as a "Trainee Chemist". It was either this or start working in a Bank, the only other prospect available at the time, and that I couldn't handle. I did like Chemistry at school, and mention it, because later in life, I would become a Chemistry teacher, the one thing at school I never believed I would ever become, a bloody teacher.

But you never know life had planned for you.

Back to today….
It's now seven days since I got the news about the Cancer, and I've unburdened myself, a literary enema so to speak, helping purge myself of stuff that maybe I should have got rid of a long time ago. It's not been a bad idea to look back and take stock of how far I've come since those days. It's made me appreciate more how good my life has really been… .

One visitor today, my mate Chris, but otherwise the phone has been very quiet, no get well cards through the letter box, because the world has gone back to normal, *or was it the one day postal strike.*

 I'm not sure.

Helen is sitting at the table, doing her school records and it sort of feels everything has gone back to normal for the first time in a very long week, it really does.

I'm calling it the end of phase one, the shock for everyone, and the dealing with it phase.

And I'm glad.

One week gone, inside I'm good, apart from the odd "House" moment which I know will come along when I least expect it, and still very aware that the time, from now, until the operation, is getting shorter.
Alex named it in one the other day. He said to Laura," Your dad's lucky, he doesn't have to fight Cancer, he's just getting it cut out. All he has to do is recover from an operation".

Little mantras like this do help!

And I wish I'd never written about the washing up and Cancer thing yesterday, because guess who did the washing up tonight?

Serves me right!

<u>Day Eight – Tuesday 3rd July 2007.</u>

There are over forty Indian Restaurants in Leeds, and
according to the tourist information, fifty nine are situated in
Bradford, the official, "Curry capital of Britain", in 2004. So a
bomb attack at Leeds / Bradford airport would be a bit like an
own goal. It would be easy to spot though,

*The suicide bombers would be in white coats and
stethoscopes, seeing as the N.H.S. is now the latest training
ground for terrorists, at least I think that's what the papers
are trying to tell us…*

But the top news today is that Kylie is back. God I've missed
her! I've thought about her recently, not in the usual lustful,
heavy breathing way, 'cos she is gorgeous, but, as you know,
she's had Cancer too.

Isn't she brilliant?

It's also raining again, but it wasn't this morning when I went
"Crutching"

Have you ever learnt how to use a pair of crutches? Looks
easy yeah?
Oh, no it isn't!
I have, of course, been practicing on the stairs, in the house,
but outside, in the big bad world, it's a whole new ball game.
Time takes on a whole new meaning.
First of all……*It takes forever to get anywhere*!
Fifteen minutes to go a mere three hundred yards to the Ladies
Hairdressers, and yes, I find a ladies hairdresser is much better
than a Gent's barber, because there's a lot more gossip,
Crossing a road is just plain suicidal.

Then there are the little things that normal able bodied people never think about. The council do not make pavements flat, like the living room, and roads have curves in them, so where to cross takes a great deal of thought. It takes planning and forethought to go anywhere, and by adding in road junctions, drain covers, and pot-holes, a walk to the shop turns the whole thing into something like an assault course.

My arms and shoulders are seriously aching, as is my good left leg, and my left foot has just gone dead.

The right leg is fine because it's been pretending it isn't there.

I got back home exhausted and shaking like a dog's back leg. I sat down in my big comfy chair, and slept for over an hour!

Claire the physiotherapist said to practice and now I know why.

She's a bloody Sadist!

Whether it will do any good in the long run, I guess I'll have to wait and see.

This afternoon, I popped in to see the Mother in law, but she'd just gone out to "Weight Watchers", and why a seventy six year old lady goes to a weight loss club is beyond me. I suppose if Eddie's Viagra is that good......enough!....there are some images a son-in-law should not have in his mind!

But the parrot was there, an African Grey.

We had a bit of a chat, at least the parrot did, a*nd there I was, all alone with a parrot, a pair of crutches, and the moment felt a little bit strange all of a sudden! All I needed was a cutlass and an eye patch, oooh aaargh! Weird!*

I'm in a good mood today! It's been confirmed that The Boy is landing at Leeds / Bradford Airport tomorrow. I'm all excited.

It's time to reminisce again, and you'll be glad to know that the next bit is a lot more cheerful.

I met Helen, the love of my life when I was nineteen, at a party. Not quite a lightning bolt across a crowded room, more of a, *"Can you take Helen outside because she's going to be sick"*, kind of moment.

So I did.

We got married when we were twenty-five, and in the six years in between meeting and marriage, we had more ups and downs than a pair of tart's knickers! Looking back, we were always in love, I would even say from that very first day. "Her indoors!", "Our lass", "Her who thinks she should be obeyed "….*is and has always been, my soul mate.*
But in the early days, it wasn't easy, we've both been born under the sign of Gemini, and four very stubborn people living under the same roof is always going to cause problems. In those early years, we really couldn't handle it!

Our Claire reckons I was just plain lucky," 'cos mum was pretty good looking and a bit of a catch, and let's face it Dad, you were nothing special".

I think she was probably right.

We met at Bingley College, lovingly referred to by many students as, "Bingley College of Knowledge", an isolated teacher training establishment on the edge of Ilkley Moor, the same Ilkley Moor that gave us the famous "Where has tha' been since I saw thee?" song.

My education took place mainly in or around the College bar, on our regular rugby trips, and involved consuming copious amounts of subsidized beer in my attempt to become an educated man. But the icing on the cake was finding out that as a male student, I was outnumbered about four to one by females. Magic!

While it never had the reputation of being an Oxford or Cambridge centre of academic excellence, it's worth pointing out that in the mid seventies, Bingley College hit the press as being *the first Educational establishment in the Country that had mixed accommodation*. Five halls of Residence, one men's, and four women's, all connected by an underground tunnel which "The Sun" referred to as "The Tunnel of Love". You could keep your Oxbridge degrees, Bingley was the place for me.

I was in Heaven and went mad, and for three years, I studied P.E. at what must have been the worst P.E. college in the country, and had a ball. It was said that P.E. students left Bingley with the "three B's", a bird, a B.Ed, and a Beer Belly", and it wasn't far wrong.

But what it did do was turn out good teachers.

Rugby and football trips to other colleges were the highlights of the week, and very often ended up with the traditional kidnap, when we used to grab a couple of unsuspecting members of the opposite team, after the traditional drinking competitions, and bring them back to Bingley on the coach. To begin with, our victim would usually put up a fight until they all of a sudden realized how many women we had on the bus, and amazingly enough, soon calmed down.
We had one bloke who stayed with us for three days, and then kept coming back over the next few months for more of what Bingley had to offer.

And I can't ever think about my time here without thinking about John Newnes!

What a man! His party trick was a wonder to behold!

After the game, it was a quick shower, and then straight to the College bar for, amidst much singing, the traditional tribal activities. mainly the drinking competitions, *and if memory serves me correctly, during all of that time, we never ever lost!* Our ace up the sleeve was Newnsie! If it ever looked like the opposition were getting close to beating us, we'd bring out John.

His party trick was to shove a piece of string up his nose with a biro, cough, and lo and behold, the string would appear out of his mouth.

He'd then pull either end while we rolled about in laughter, mainly at the shocked look on the faces of the other college. John had had a Public School Education, so I needn't say much more here.

But it wasn't all singing and dancing. Actually it was….but I once had to go and see Tom Price, our well loved Dean of Students over a few serious matters.

"Thanks for coming Billy. I wonder if you could help me out with a few things?"

"I'll do my best Tom!" said I.

"We've had a couple of complaints Billy."

"I'm sorry to hear that Tom." I replied.

"Last Thursday, someone climbed up the clock tower at around two o'clock in the morning and changed the times on the clocks."

"I know Tom, I slept in this morning!"

"And someone went back up again last night and took down the Flag, (this was around the time of the Queen's Jubilee), then climbed up onto the Principle's roof, put it on his TV aerial."

"Wow!" said I knowing then I was in deep doo doo.

"I've also had a report that you've been living illegally in the Halls of Residence for the past nine months?"

You could say I'd gone quiet by now!

"The cleaners have also asked if you can stop riding your Honda Fifty up and down the tunnel."

"Sorry Tom!"

"And one more thing Billy!", and I thought, that's it, I'm dead. Any future I've possibly had in Education was this very moment, is spinning uncontrollably down the drain.

"I've just bought a house in the Lake's, near Keswick, and I know that you come from Whitehaven, so if you need a lift home any Friday, the offer's there! What a man!

They were three brilliant years. I worked every holiday, Xmas's were spent working in Hotels in the Lake District where I'd get a job as a barman, rather than go back to another miserable Whitehaven Christmas.
The shit on the toilet seat was very vivid for a long time.

My other holidays were spent working on building sites, and because of this, I'd return to college loaded. I usually felt like a millionaire when I got eventually got back to good old Bingley.

The one exception was on waking up on Xmas day in a Hotel in Windermere, itching like hell and covered in bites. I'd caught Scabies off the disgusting staff bed, and this the only four star hotel in Windermere. It took me seven hours to hitch hike to Whitehaven on Christmas day, looking through windows at families eating Xmas dinner, thinking here we go again.

I hated Xmas! I raced back to Bingley, and Helen, for the New Year.

At the end of this period, we both qualified as Teachers, Helen teaching Infant children, with me taking over when the creatures turned a little more human and reached Secondary school.

But I didn't teach for the first ten years. Firstly, there were no jobs and secondly, *teaching was the last thing I wanted to do*! Someone had given me the advice that you can't be "A proper Teacher", without learning something about the real world, a truth I see everyday in schools, because, in my not so humble opinion, too many teachers have never left school.

And thirdly, I wanted an adventure!

All in all, this hasn't been a bad day.

Today's news.
Alan Johnston is free at last. One hundred and fourteen days in
captivity, and at last, he's free to be with his loved ones.
Brilliant news! His mum and dad were being interviewed, by
the BBC, and they were so excited. His dad certainly was
because his poor old mum couldn't get a word in!

I know exactly how he feels. My boy came home today.

We'd had a lazy morning, mainly because the "Crutching" had
left my chest and arms in tatters, and a mantra inside my head
was chanting, *"Don't train on tired muscles"*.
So, having a valid excuse for not sweating too much today, we
had a walk on the beach, watched some kids being introduced
to the joys of surfing in kayaks, watched the fishing cobbles
being dragged up the beach, and had a cup of tea. Fairly
normal really, fairly chilled out, no get well cards in the post,
and only one phone call from my mate Peter, the night before.

Wazzaaaaarh! When Peter phones, we become Budweiser
Frogs! Don't ask why!

So, there we are, back home after our lovely walk, all ready to
leave for Leeds / Bradford Airport, and Helen sees there's a
message on the answer machine.
"Dad, it's your Son here." Did I mention he was a bright boy?
Now who could that be I wonder?

"Don't bother coming to Leeds /Bradford, I won't be
there….", and the rest was garbled. Helen sort of panicked a
bit and pressed a button to try and replay the message,
unfortunately *the delete button*. We have another "Oh bugger"
moment….bugger!

Cutting a very long story short, Andy was eventually escorted onto a flight to Manchester landing at nine p.m. that evening. I drove over to pick him up and find airport security in Manchester still very tight, despite the reduced threat alert from the Glasgow bomb attempt. It was all a bit chaotic.

Eventually, he comes through passport control, and the drama of the day was immediately forgotten.

It was good to see him! *Ok, more than good!*

I drove on my own to Manchester because felt I needed some space, and felt I needed some time to be on my own with my thoughts. I guess I thought that it would also give us some time together on the way back, just the two of us, with no fuss, to explain the situation, and I could start the reassuring process. We popped into see our Laura seeing as she only lives ten minutes away from the Airport, or, taking my short cut, about thirty five minutes away. They had a big, big hug, (well she is his little/big sister) and we finally got home about midnight.

I know he's worried, because he stayed awake in the car, talking all the way home, which is something he just doesn't do....The Boy can sleep for England!

Straight away, mum put his trainers into the washing machine because they stank, and put them in again the following morning because they were still a hazard to health. They had a big, big hug.

So where are we today.... We're now into phase two, the phase of acceptance, of reassurance, back in the shelter of my home, surrounded by a loving family, and maybe a little bit of denial is setting in.

You see, *it all feels so normal.*

I've sort of got a routine going, getting up and seeing what's on the news, writing up the events of the day before, putting today's memories into some sort of order, sorting out today's healthy meals, and organizing what exercises to do today. I am having no discomfort whatsoever, and as I've mentioned, the phone has been very quiet for the past few days, Life has gone back to the way it was, not only for me, but for all concerned.

Cancer's a strange thing. When my mate Doren had Lung Cancer, I found it difficult to deal with. I phoned regularly, but didn't visit as often as I should have, because deep down I was in denial and was convinced that she would pull through. I didn't know what to say and I suppose selfishly, I wanted to remember her as she was, not as she may become towards the end.

I suppose what I'm trying to say is that although the phone's gone quieter of late, I hope it doesn't stay that way for long because I honestly feel my situation is very temporary as nowhere near as serious or severe as Doren's eventually became.

But thought's like these do come visiting!

Besides, the idea of facing one's own mortality isn't anything new.

I remember when I had the Heart attack when I was forty years old, and looking back, it came with so many positives. But at the time, when I was a bit low, I remember thinking, in the first few days of my recovery, and whilst I was still a bit scared, *that it wasn't fair*, because I was too young for this, and didn't want to leave Helen and the kids. They were far too young to be left without a Dad, *it just wouldn't be fair.*

I remember doing the nearest thing to prayer I've ever done, and, while laying in bed all alone, said something along the lines of " This isn't fair, and if there actually is anything or anyone out there listening to this, at least give me the time to see my kids become the Adults I can be proud of".

So right now, I'm thinking that I've had that time, and they are the "Adults I can be proud of "and if things did go bums down, well then, how could I complain?.

But I would complain.

I really do believe I've been given a second chance, because as the Doctor said, if you have to have Cancer, this is the one to have, it grows slow, it's been caught early, chop it out, rebuild, and off you go again. I am getting a bit sick of the Bionic man jokes though.

I need to be around to look after Helen in old age, hers, not mine, especially where the car is concerned.

Why are there so many funny stories about women drivers?

Helen is a good driver…. Honest!.

She occasionally "grazes" the car, but nothing serious. Men bash or dent cars, but Helen grazes hers. All our cars have grazes.

However, when she initially passed her driving test, I did have my concerns. The day she passed her test, she was eight months pregnant with Andrew, and was massive!

The Examiner had her drive round the maternity hospital five times in case she went into labour.

Anyhow, about a year later, we were traveling over Holme Moss, a moorland road the other side of Huddersfield , with a sheer drop on one side, my side, just as the Sun was setting, and darkness was settling in.

I remember a car coming towards us, and *Helen turned off the lights*!

"WHAT ARE YOU DOING?", I calmly whispered into her ear, bottom tightly clenched.

"I'm dipping my headlights", she replied.

Mind you, a teacher mate of mine, Rob Morris, trumped that when he told me the story of his wife. She'd just got a new car, and went to the local garage for the first time. All excited, she checked the oil, checked the fluid levels, and then checked the tyres. She then thought, I'd better change the Air in the tyres, and then let them all down!

It was then she found out that the air compressor, to blow them back up again,had broken down!

But Helen is a good driver! Honest.

In the Daily Express this morning, I read the following :-
"In a Sainsbury's sponsored survey, of sixteen to nineteen year olds, the following was discovered :-
Less than 50% of people had had Steak and Kidney pie.
Less than 50% of people had had Clotted Cream.

And less than 45% of people had had Spotted Dicks.

It sort of made me chuckle.

And, in my first week of careful dieting, I've lost five pounds.

Not as much as Pavarotti!

I was saddened to read that the great man himself is down to a mere eleven stone, fourteen stone lighter than this time last year, but unfortunately it's not down to any new amazing diet. The poor man has pancreatic cancer, but his brave fight continues. I hope he makes it.

It's bloody everywhere! It's like buying a new burgundy Ford Focus. You didn't even notice they existed before you bought one, but now that you've got one, they're everywhere, and it's a bit like that. Everywhere I look, there's Cancer.

I'm lucky, mines only got another two or three weeks before it's gone.

We got up late, from the traveling yesterday, and went into Scarborough to have a light lunch with Claire. We're not missing a minute together, and she wanted to make sure the boy was ok, and give him, yes you've got it, a big, big hug!.

We had to buy our Andrew some new trainers!

Two spins in the washing machine just wasn't enough for them to pass any kind of Health and Safety regulation.

More reminiscing, and not too depressing....honest.

I'd left Bingley College as a qualified teacher, and the only thing I knew, was that the last thing I felt competent to do, or wanted to do was teach, at least not just yet.

There was a world out there waiting, and I wanted an adventure.

I spent a little time doing some supply teaching work, youth club work, and a few other jobs, but I wanted, needed something different.
Helen and I were having what can best be described as a fluid relationship, with totally different agenda's and had, once again, fallen out big time.
She'd gone off to Athens to work as a Governess, and I eventually made the decision to go after her.

I'd never left the UK before, so you can imagine my excitement!

I took my last £100 out of the bank, went to the Post Office and bought a one year passport. I then went to the Army and Navy stores and bought a cheap tent, and a rucksack, and set off to hitchhike to Greece, first stop Amsterdam via North Sea Ferries from Hull.
Hitchhiking in those days was quite common. Students and service personnel could always be seen thumbing for lifts at motorway roundabouts, it was sort of accepted. Besides, apart from being cheaper, it was usually faster than public transport. I loved thumbing lifts.

While I was sitting at the bar on the ship, a kindly coach driver named Andy offered me a lift up to Amsterdam, just himself, his brother Pete, and *forty three women from a pub in Filey.* Happy days!

After a weekend of clog factories, cheese factories, bars, more bars, and a brilliant day at the Heineken Brewery, three days after arriving in Amsterdam, I finally waved goodbye to Andy and my new friends. Unfortunately, by now, I was down to less than £20, so got a job in a local paper factory to save enough money to carry on to Greece. (No, it didn't blow about in the wind....paper factory...get it?).

Once I'd got back up to the £100, which took the best part of two months, because I was just having too much fun, I set off once more to hitchhike to Athens. The trip took six days and was fairly uneventful, apart from being arrested along with two German lads at the border crossing for smuggling drugs, them not me. After a night in the cells, I was on my way again after they'd admitted I was just a passenger.

It was also uneventful, despite being in a wagon for three days, with Bruno, the masturbating Italian lorry driver who had this way of driving down the road with one hand on the wheel, and one hand on his... I'm sure you get the drift. It was a good job he wore a big jumper. Going into Italy, he even handed his passport out of the window with his driving hand, his left hand never missing a beat, for want of a better word.

Once over the Italian border, via the Mont Blanc tunnel, Bruno bought me my first Italian spaghetti and we had a very pleasant meal. Before sitting down to eat, I noticed he washed his hands very thoroughly.

When I left him the next day, we shook hands, (and yes, I was fairly sure that he had just washed them that morning) and his last words were, "Beely, if you ever need a lift up to Paris...."

Not bloody likely!

I thumbed my way down Italy, and caught a ferry from Ancona to Patras, to meet Helen in the centre of Athens, six days after setting off from Amsterdam.

"God, you stink!", were her first loving words, "you're not coming back to the house with me looking like that!" She was obviously glad to see me!

To make things more convenient, I booked into a cheap travelers hostel down in the Plaka, got cleaned up, and we had what I remember as four very lovely days, eating in cheap tavernas, wandering around the Acropolis as the Sun was setting, just lovely.
Unfortunately, by now, the money was starting to run out again, so it was time to look for work, and somewhere back in Holland, I'd heard it was fairly easy to get a job crewing on yachts out of Pireaus. This seemed a cool idea, because it included a roof over my head, and three meals a day, and some money, so off I went and found a job on a beautiful 1936 racing yacht which was heading to Turkey.

Two weeks later, I was back in Athens because they wouldn't let me into Turkey with a one year passport, and I was turned back at the border, with enough money for about another three or four days with Helen. I was having an adventure and discovered that finding work on the yachts was easy to get through a bar in Pireaus called the Plum Pudding, where boats advertised on a notice board when crew were needed.

My next trip was a seventeen day charter from Pireaus, round the Ionian islands to Corfu, which was seventeen days of pure bliss. Every day we'd snorkel for hours, and every evening we'd pull into a small harbour, and once the work was done, washing down the yacht, and getting ready for the following day, we'd visit a taverna by the harbour,(every island has one), and watch the Sun go down, all the while eating amazing food washed down with the local Retzina.

Once I reached Corfu, I felt it was time to leave, get a flight back to Athens, and you've guessed it, another three or four days with Helen.

Then it became a bit more serious, the sailing, not the relationship.

A luxury motor yacht, formally owned by the Sultan of Oman, needed two crew members.

"Have you ever done any Silver service waitering?" I was asked in what was the nearest thing to an interview I'd had so far.

"Yes, I've worked in some of the best hotels in England," I reply, not mentioning the Scabies, and the fact that it only lasted one day.
"Fine! Congratulations then, you now have the position of Chief Steward. Can you be in Dubrovnik the day after tomorrow? Good. Pop back in tomorrow afternoon and pick up your airline tickets."

Sounded brilliant, but I had a slight problem. I'd ran out of money, and didn't have a full passport, a problem because I knew I couldn't get into what was the former Yugoslavia with a one year passport.

I raced up to Athens, straight to the British Consulate, and filled the forms in for the full passport. While they were being processed, I suddenly realized I hadn't enough money to pay for it, and after much pleading with the lady doing the processing to hold onto it for a couple of hours, and that I'd be back with the money soon, I flew out the door, ran three miles to Helen's employer's only to find out that she wasn't there. I borrowed the money off her boss, and ran the three miles back to the Consulate where I eventually paid for my new ten year passport with ten minutes to spare. I then almost passed out with heat exhaustion.

Helen and I spent my last night in a hotel near the Airport and the following morning I flew to Dubrovnik, where I came into contact with a different breed of people altogether, money people. Don't forget, I'd come straight off a council estate in the north of England, and had never met a millionaire before. I had no idea what to expect.
The first lot I encountered were probably best described as what used to be called "nouveaux riches", a bunch of arrogant self made American arseholes who simply thought that the world had been made just for them. They complained over the least little thing, the food, the weather, the boat, everything, and I'm convinced to this day, that the "wives", were a couple of supposedly high class hookers, because they looked like they'd been around a bit if you catch my drift.

Despite this, it was still a memorable trip, and for the next three weeks, we sailed round what are now the Croatian islands, before ending up in Venice. My first sight of Venice was sailing up the Grand Canal after an overnight crossing, with the Sun just beginning to rise over St Mark's Square, absolutely beautiful. Unfortunately, I soon began to hate the place, because it then rained continuously for the three days we were there, everything was rip off expensive, and the canals stank of raw sewage. It didn't help when my first foot in Venice slipped while getting off the boat, and I went straight up to my neck into the Grand Canal!

I have returned to Venice a couple of times since, and have fallen totally in love with the place.

The arseholes eventually left, and we moved the yacht on to Trieste for the next couple of weeks before sailing south to Brindisi in the south of Italy.

After six weeks though, I'd had enough, and was missing Helen, so I sort of jumped ship, and made my way to Kefalonia, where Helen had relocated with the family for the summer holidays.

This time I stayed for an Idyllic ten days, sleeping on the beach, and spending every day swimming, snorkeling, living off fresh bread, local cheese and tomatoes. For some reason, the family had started calling me "The English Zorba", which I'm hoping was a term of endearment.

Most nights, Helen and I would go to a little taverna on the cliff top, where the two of us would eat traditional Greek food, while watching the Sun set, then head back to the beach for some swimming and some serious snogging. (I use the word snogging very very loosely. My kids could be reading this someday.)

But once again, the money began running out and so it was back to the Plum Pudding for my next adventure.I hadn't realized it at the time, but I would continue to find work from bars for the next three years.

I landed my next job on a top luxury yacht called "The Southern Breeze", a beautiful fifty five *metre* motor yacht that had taken two months to sail across the Atlantic, just to give the owners a three week holiday round the Greek islands, and these people were a different class altogether, "supermillionaires".

What lovely people they were.

Despite the trappings of wealth which they had obviously been born to, they were very genuine people. We met them in three hired limousines at the Airport in Athens, after they'd flown in on private jets, and we were kitted out in full regalia, white shirts, bow ties and all, to chauffeur them directly to the yacht.

To give you an idea of how rich this guy was, the owner had just bought a new toy, *a cigarette speedboat, from the team that had won the world championship that year,* and its speed on water was amazing.

Once on board, it was very different, very much more relaxed, but still hard work nonetheless.

They were also a very interesting bunch of people to watch too.

The first week that they were on board, the atmosphere was like anyone else the first week of their holiday. They'd be smiling, relaxing, and spent hours playing on windsurfers, water skiing, etc etc, but I soon noticed that once we got into week two, boredom was setting in, and by week three, we were constantly going to the nearest island with an airport so they could fly out again. They got bored easily and didn't have to put up with it. I found it a bit sad really.

My memories around this time include sailing away from the Holy mountain of Mount Athos, where no woman had set foot for the last two thousand years, just as the Sun was setting which was amazing in it's colour and spirituality, and, on another occasion, sailing to a prohibited area of the Aegean Sea, where the owner and his guests went diving, bringing back a whole load of Greek Urns and artefacts and hiding them in the hold, before eventually taking them back to the States.

My fellow stewards were a pair of aggressive homosexual blokes, whose best mate was the chef. The three of them were often found late at night hanging out at the end of the pier, looking for young greek boys to play with. It was a different world to any I'd known before. They once told me that they were saving their money to go back to Florida to visit an auction where they would bid for what could be best described as a well oiled Chippendale,..... and I don't mean a sideboard or wardrobe.

This had been a good trip, but once we'd reached Pireaus it was back to Athens as usual but summer was coming to an end, and Helen and I once more had a major bust up.

I'd had enough of Greece and it was time to hitchhike back to England, with Helen due to come home three weeks later.

It was back on the road again.
I left Greece by ferry to Ancona, and fifty two hours after disembarking in Italy I walked through our front door in Whitehaven, having spent four pounds and fifty pence in total. I'd stowed away on the North Sea Ferry, and landed back home, in England, with the grand sum of around ninety six pounds, four pounds less than I'd started with seven months previously, and knew straight away I'd made a major, major mistake in coming back home.

Three days later I went to stay with our Beverley who was living in Redcar, where I was simply miserable for the next two months, until Helen finally arrived home.

But by that time I'd had enough of waiting for her to return.

We met up for one miserable wet night in York Railway Station, where things definitely weren't right between us, and the day after, I was on my way back to Holland to become "A Cowboy."

Back to today....

Today ended in a really happy buoyant mood. We all sat in front of the TV and watched, "Casino Royale", a good film, but in my opinion, not a good James Bond film.

We had a lazy tea, buying a couple of cooked chickens and some salads from the Supermarket.

"There you go Dad," remarked Claire, "you've got two chicken boobs."

"Cheeky sod!"

I've just received the following text:-

"Wanted! Middle Eastern Doctor with burning ambition to work in the N.H.S."

Naughty, naughty…

Today is the opening of the Tour de France, in London, first stage of the Tour being next Sunday, from London to Canterbury. I'm not sure why it is starting in England when it's the Tour de France….it's a bit like having the F.A. cup Final in Wales, or the Rugby League Challenge Cup Final in Scotland which seems to have happened a lot in recent years.

It just doesn't seem right somehow….

The motivation music of the day was the theme music from the film, "Flashdance". I can still see in my mind Jennifer Beale diving through the air in black leotard and stockings in her audition scene, only apparently it wasn't her, it was a French professional dancer and anyhow, who cares, I found it very moving.

My training today consisted of another hour "Crutching", round the village, and twenty minutes on the spinning bike, and I felt great!

It can only be a matter of time before "Crutching" takes over from aerobics, or aqua-robics or whatever the latest exercise fad is today, it's got everything. It gives you upper bodyand leg strength, (ok, only the one leg at present.), and *it's incredibly sociable*. Little old ladies flatten themselves against walls so that I can pass, and smile, even after I've pointed out that I'm just practicing. (I'm a bit frightened of old ladies' smiles. I think it's the amount of loose skin that sort of hangs down from the mouth. It's easy to see why babies cry when old ladies stick their faces in their prams.)

It's another world, the world of Crutching. People stop you in the street and start up conversations. Actually, it's usually other "Crutchers", people in wheelchairs, and folk on those little motorized mobility buggy things who stop, or pull in, and share their stories with you.

"Hip or knee, lad?", was the first question today from a chappy who was standing, loading his wheelchair into the back of his car, though I did wonder why did he needed a wheelchair when he had a car, but I'm new at this and soon figured it out.

"I'm only practicing actually", I sort of sheepishly reply.

"Knees are worse son", he continued, oblivious to what I'd just said.
The guy on the motorized harley was funnier. His advice was "I wouldn't go to the Pub on those if I were you....", and then continued by pointing out that Pubs aren't the same anymore, especially since smoking was banned and I had to wonder if smoking and visiting pubs wasn't what made him need his Harley in the first place...

It's very surreal!

Chris came round tonight with some stuff designed to boost my immune system, Garlic, Vitamin C tablets, Echinacea, and something called Goji berries, a true miracle food. Chris is a former teaching colleague and my cycling mate, and has taken on the mantle of cheering me up and keeping me going. He's doing a good job.

Soon the conversation got on to aftercare and what to expect in the weeks after the Operation, and Chris knows about this. A few years ago, we cycled up the Tourmalet in the Pyrenees, and on the way down, Chris came off. An Irish girl, who witnessed what happened at the time, told me,

" Sure, and I knew he was English. From the way he said, *SHIT!,* as he flew through the air!"

Luckily, he wrapped himself around a tree, sustaining a spinal injury, and I say luckily because beyond the tree was a sheer drop. He was airlifted to Hospital by helicopter, returned to the UK by air ambulance, and then spent the next four months recovering, hence the expertise!

We're still planning how to sneak his bike past his wife Sheila, so we can go back and finish the job, because we sort of have a rule that says, you can't bag the hill unless you get up and down again, and he only got up !"

The conversation then got on to Macmillan's nurses, commodes, banister rails, toilet seat cushions.

Suitably cheered up, I had an early night with a book.

Day Twelve – Saturday 7th July 2007.

And now the Prologue:-.... *Haven't I already done that?*

Today's the biggest day in the British sporting Calendar, with the Tour de France Prologue taking place in London for the very first time, Women's final day at Wimbledon, (Is it still going on? I thought it had finished ages ago!), and of course the British Grand Prix qualifiers, where I believe the favorite to win tomorrow is a twelve year old Louis Hamilton.

And this morning, I just don't care. I've hardly slept for thinking about bloody commodes! I'm having a bad hair day! Unfortunately, the sunshine has done nothing to brighten my mood, because I'm simply pissed off today.

It probably started after Chris's visit yesterday, might even be the Goji berries, I'm not sure.

Today I'm just pissed off.

When I started to put this book together, I sort of gave myself the three to four weeks time period, based on the waiting time to "O" day, operation day, which is roughly twenty five days in total. That makes today theoretically the half way stage, so I'm now in the run in period, and maybe that's what I can put today's miserable mood down to, I'm not at all sure.

Or it could be that our Andrew isn't quite there yet, very nearly, but not yet through his phase one so to speak. Don't get me wrong, he's nearly there, but he's also halfway through his time here before he gets back to Greece, so I'm thinking that although getting back to his version of normal is without doubt what's best for him, until next October, I'll miss him.

It could also very be that I feel Helen is moving into phase three, the "it's time to get worried stage", and I'm still happily plodding on in phase two.

You see, when Helen's stressed, she becomes logical, and today she became logical.

It was time to put the house in order, sort out a new mobile phone contract, check the last three months' bank statements, organize the campervan for it's MOT, check all the Insurance documents to see if we're spending money needlessly, and shred any paperwork that some villain might get hold of, and clear the bank accounts. (He can willingly have my overdraft!).

The point is, THESE ARE MY JOBS! I'm the logical one, I keep a scanning eye on the state of the family finances, not brilliantly, I might add, more of an overview, and it's the way I've done things for the last twenty seven years. I also intend to KEEP MY JOBS!, because *I'm not going anywhere*!

Helen is worried, and naturally so. She's also started bringing up the aftercare situation, but *in phase two, there's no need to do these jobs just yet, they're phase three jobs. I don't need to worry about all this stuff just yet….*

Chris very kindly offered to put in some stair rails in the downstairs toilet, and has offered us the use of his toilet seat extension, so I got pictures in my head of me sitting on the Loo, doing the crossword, with my legs dangling like a little boy's.. "Should we get in touch with the hospital yet to organize some sort of special reclining bed, an upright chair and, God forbid, a commode?", went the conversation.
I was always very serious about the bowel movements!

And Hugh Laurie hasn't helped, the bastard!

House has gone and been diagnosed with Cancer and I didn't see it coming.

The "House", quote for today was, "Once you tell, then every conversation from then on is about Cancer."
I turned it off. I'm not watching "House" anymore, it's too damned depressing, and I've just bloody well ordered the box set of Series One, to watch in the hospital on my new DVD player.

But it's true, I know it is! It's no different from having a Heart Attack!

I remember reading somewhere that after a heart attack happens, a day doesn't go by without you thinking about it. Every day, and I do mean every single day, there are a few moments, albeit brief moments, when you think...." Is today going to be the day?", because you are sort of convinced that your eventual demise is going to be from another Heart Attack, even though it makes no logical sense. The only exception to the rule has been the last twelve days!

And so, am I doomed to be thinking and talking with everyone I meet solely about the topic of Cancer. (No, not the tropic of cancer, that's something else!).

So all in all, I've had something of a bad day. This is despite knowing that I have had the best years of my life post heart attack, wearing lycra, ten years of running, cycling, white water kayaking, and best of all, watching my kids grow up etc etc. , and despite knowing that in reality, should all go well, I'll be rid of my Cancer in just over two or three weeks from now.

I did say I would be honest, so yes, it's been a bad day. It's a few hours on, and I now feel a little silly.

I've just seen the end of House, and he doesn't have Cancer, he was faking it, in other words it's gone. In a strange sort of way, I feel better!

But I still need cheering up and a visit to the Cinema seems like a good idea.

"Do you want me to drive?" asks Helen.

"No, I do not! I'm not a bloody invalid yet!" I sort of yelled, and I know it wasn't fair, or kind, but did I mention, *I was having a bad day?*

So we trooped off to the Cinema in York to see the new "Shrek" movie, and though not as good as "Shreks one and two", it did the trick. What was surprising was how many single adults were in there, mainly blokes.

They can't all be perverts, can they? It wasn't that long ago that you used to have to kidnap nieces and nephews, or best friend's kids to watch a movie like this.

How the world has changed.

We got home after Eleven. I went to bed, and slept like a baby!

<u>Day Thirteen - Sunday 8th July 2007.</u>

Yet another beautiful morning in the Vale of York!

I went through to Scarborough to pick our Claire up for Sunday lunch, and the seafront at Scarborough was absolutely jam packed with holidaymakers enjoying the summer weather, sitting in deckchairs, kids on rides, and not a cloud in the sky..

It threw it down an hour later, but today I don't care, I'm feeling better!

It's Sunday. There was nothing much on the news today, unless of course you count Venus Williams winning again at Wimbledon, or more news about the War on terror. So, like I said, there was no real news today!

I'm thinking of stopping the news reports until something new turns up, it's all a bit recycled.

Today was a lovely day. We had lunch at the Pub, Claire, Andrew, Helen and myself, and, despite the "fight on flab", (incidentally another three pounds off!), I thoroughly enjoyed a decent meal, and a glass of wine.

I spent the afternoon watching the Tour de France on Eurosport, Roger Federer won Wimbledon again, *and Louis Hamilton was beaten into third place in the British Grand Prix, by two grown ups in faster cars.*

Later in the afternoon, Bob came round, with wife Heather, and showed me his scars. It's funny what people do to cheer you up, isn't it!

Bob and Heather are both very strong Christians, and I've known them for years, or more accurately, Helen has, so, whenever I'm in the room, the topic of Christianity never comes up.

He's also a retired English teacher, and he kindly looked over my inane ramblings, and gave me a bit of a boost with both encouragement and advice.

Actually, I was impressed with his scars, because they were way smaller than I had expected when he started to drop his trousers, and not where I thought they would be, actually in a much less obvious place. I'm thinking that maybe it would be a good idea to find out more about the up and coming operation but quite honestly, I don't know if I want to know the ins and outs of what I will be going through. Maybe ignorance is bliss, and I'll be better sitting back and leaving it to the experts. Bob has had two hip replacement operations, the both of them being done at the same time, so we had long conversations on the topic of scars, morphine, bowel movements, and other appropriate after dinner topics.
It was quite reassuring!

So, here's some more of the life story, my "Auf Wiedersehn pet" years, and probably the craziest time of my life.

"Holland doesn't have Cowboys", I hear you say.

"Oh yes it does!" Or it certainly did in the late seventies and eighties. Ok, maybe not the "yahooing", horse riding variety, but Holland was full of Cowboys,

I know, because I became one.

What I'm referring to as a Cowboy , is a "chancer", an unskilled bloke, working as a tradesman, without having gone through any unnecessary training or apprenticeship.

108

Holland in the seventies was booming! Oil and Gas refineries were being thrown up all over the place, and there weren't enough skilled men to fill the jobs, leaving lots of opportunities for the Cowboys. I became a Cowboy lagger. (More explaining needed. A Lagger lags pipes, and is a more accurate term than "Thermal Insulation Engineer", the official title. He wraps pipes in insulating material, usually mineral wool or fibre glass which itches like hell, then covers it in a sheet metal wrap for protection.) It is a tough, physical job, can be a very dirty job, but is a very well paid job.

"Any Laggers in the bar", shouts the Barman.

"Over here mate!", I reply, not sure what a Lagger is at this time, but if you don't take a chance…

"Gulf Refinery tomorrow morning lad, van will pick you up outside the bar at seven, ok?"

"Sound", I reply, then phoned up Bev's husband, Robert, the brother in law, who was a lagger, to find out what the hell a lagger was and what it was he did.

I survived the first week, mainly because I was looked after by the other lads on the site. What I discovered, was that there was a real camaraderie among the men I was working with, and the other lads helped me to get to grips with how to do the job. I later found out that most of them were Cowboys too, and so, once you had sort of shown you were willing to work hard, and had picked up some basic skills, you were looked after, and you looked after others.
At the end of the week, I was given more money that I could have earned in a month teaching, and it hadn't been too hard. No marking, no unnecessary meetings, and no being looked at nastily because you'd been sitting in someone else's chair in the staffroom nonsense, I knew I was on to a winner.

Add on the fact the world was becoming more energy conscious after the oil embargo's of the early seventies, and things looked pretty good.

I was sacked the following week.

But I had picked up enough to try again the following day, kept persevering and I became a lagger.

The next three years were spent traveling around Northern Europe, working on Oil Refineries around Amsterdam, Rotterdam, and Hamburg, earning what I thought was big money, and spending it just as quickly, having a freedom I'd never known before. But the big bonus were the characters I met, my fellow Cowboys, who made life sparkle with some of the antics they got up to.

I'll start off with Dougie, my best mate, and a former soldier in the RAF regiment, who had done time at Her Majesty's pleasure for something or other in his dark and distant past. I never asked because he never offered which was sort of an unwritten rule, part of the code so to speak. It made the rumours that much more mysterious.

A member of the magic circle, Dougie would constantly amazed us with his card tricks, but never ever did he do them for financial gain.
Gus was another mate who'd done fifteen years in a Glasgow jail, and always had a blade located in his belt. Both these lads turned out every night in immaculate suits, a bit like the Kray twins.

Davy and his cousin, whose name escapes me were a couple of Irish lads, who were on the run from the Irish Paramilitaries. The story went that Davy had wanted to get out of Belfast and put his past behind him. So he took some money that didn't belong to him and relocated to Holland. Again, I never asked. A few years later, un unmarked car drove past Davy's car, and put a few bullet holes into it, as a warning, as if to say, "we know where you are, just don't come back!".

Shaun was another mate. One day, Shaun disappeared off site in the van, and didn't come back. We found out later that he'd decided he needed a holiday and drove to Spain, for three weeks, at the end of which he drove back, left the van at the Ferry terminal, and went home for a break. A week later, he phoned up to say sorry, and could he have his job back?

He started work the following Monday.

Later, he decided to have another holiday, bought a car for a hundred pounds, and went to India for six months. To get back he siphoned petrol out of other cars, was caught, and locked up for two nights in the former Yugoslavia. When they eventually let him go, he went back an hour later, siphoned yet more petrol from the Police Cars, and carried on his way!

These were the characters I worked with every day. It was that kind of world, a hard working, hard drinking life, and I loved it. I was single, because Helen and I still hadn't gotten our selves sorted out yet, the money was good, and life had no real serious aspect to it.

In Rotterdam, we met for work in a local bar. If the van driver didn't turn up on time, or any of the lads had more than the usual couple of beers for breakfast, they just didn't get to work. I could handle it most of the time but we regularly had a whip round to send some of the boys back home when the hard living became too much for them to handle.

Pete Smith was the van driver, and he just didn't like going to work. One morning he came running in to the bar, and said,

" Some bastards have let all the tires down, and we can't go to work!", and that was it, another day on the ale. He later came round and whispered in everyone's ear,

"Don't let on, *it was me!*"

We already knew. We sent him home when he literally swallowed the van keys one morning, in his usual attempt to keep us in the bar all day! We all loved Pete.

One time, I remember being locked in our local bar in Rotterdam, "The Three Musketeers", by the police one night. The bloke we worked for, Bernie, had had too much to drink, and for some unbeknown reason, pulled out a loaded gun, and started waiving it at the girl behind the bar. The police were called, by which time Bernie had disappeared, and we were locked in until the early hours of the morning to give statements. From then on, Bernie used to sneak back into Holland via Belgium to keep an eye on his businesses.

On another occasion, we had to go up to Hamburg to work on a Gold refinery shutdown which was just too much for many of the boys. Whilst I was working on a pipeline, I overheard a loudspeaker message.
"Der bier wagen ist hier, der bier wagen ist hier!", which translated into, "The beer wagon is here!".
Now, I'd failed GCE German at school, but compared to the other lads, I was fluent, so I wandered down and there to my delight, was a beer wagon selling subsidized beer on site, something totally unheard of back home in England. I bought a case of beer for what was then about seven pounds fifty, ten times cheaper than what we were paying in town, thinking we'd sort of share it between ourselves.

The next thing you see is every British bloke on site running after the van for his crate of beer. It was a pantomime, with the lads coming to work fairly sober, and leaving completely battered at the end of the work day.

The lads loved Hamburg, and on occasions, like Christmas or suchlike, some of them wouldn't go home to their wives. I took Mick Clarkson to the railway station three times in three days for him to go home for Xmas. Twice, he turned up back in the bar a couple of hours later, definitely the worse for wear, and eventually, I took him onto the platform personally and poured him onto the train.

The cheap beer definitely came in very handy for my stag night.

While all this was happening, Helen and I were still having problems sorting out our relationship or whatever it had become at the time. I'd go home occasionally to see her in England, and occasionally, she'd come out to where I was working when she could.

It had gotten very murky. Just before moving up to Germany to work, Helen had phoned.

"I'm fed up of this relationship." she started.

"So am I, were getting nowhere are we?", I reply, thinking this is it, it's finally over....

"So why don't we get married?" she blurts out!

"What?"

"Get Married".

"When?"

"It's August now, so let's say November. I'll organize it, you just turn up!"

"Ok! Why not? " I remember saying, if somewhat shell shocked.

And that's what we did. I returned to England on the Thursday after two stag nights, one in Hamburg and another in Rotterdam, and had another stag night on the Friday before the wedding with my English mate Ian.

Helen had decided I needed an early night before the big day and put sleeping tablets in my coffee before I went out, but somehow, they didn't seem to work!

On the Saturday we got married, and on arrival at the Church, Helen's first words to the Minister were,

"Has he actually made it?"

She wasn't sure I'd even turn up.

(In my defence, it's fair to point out that I made it up to her in style, when I "married her" again twenty five years later, her knowing nothing about it until two hours before, but that's another story.)

After a short five day honeymoon in the Lake District, Helen and I went to back to Hamburg where we were on our way to spend our first year of marriage in what was the Sex centre of Europe, The saying, "Taking coals to Newcastle" came to mind.

While the wedding had been going on, I'd sort of forgotten to tell Helen a fairly important piece of information. *The manager on site back in Hamburg had said that if I left the job to go home, not to bother coming back, thus making me technically unemployed.* . I didn't want to spoil the wedding, so I thought it best to keep quiet about it, but I had to tell her sometime so I thought half way across the North Sea would be as good a place as any. She couldn't exactly walk out on me could she?

She wasn't happy.

The morning we got back to Hamburg, I decided that nothing ventured, nothing gained, walked straight back on site, and start working, as if nothing had happened, and, surprisingly enough, not a word was said.

We booked into a comfortable hotel while we looked for somewhere more permanent.
I'd go to work every day, come home, and we'd eat out at restaurants every night, and the honeymoon continued. It was terrific, but after a month or so though, the novelty of hotel living was wearing off, and we eventually had to think about finding somewhere else, and the only flat we could find, at what we could afford at that particular time, was smack in the middle of the Hamburg's notorious Red Light District, the Reeperbahn.

It was wall to wall hookers and a bit of a shock to Helen's system, but my lovely missus is nothing if not resilient.

Before leaving England, she'd bought a ski suit for the German winter, and was horrified to find that Hamburg's "Ladies of the night", wore these as standard issue. She got used to being propositioned on a daily basis. In fact it was a bad day when she wasn't. The Reeperbahn was eventful to say the least.

"There's someone in our Bedroom!", Helen yelled.

"Don't be so daft ", was my reply, but looked anyway, only to find a tramp asleep on the floor in our bedroom. He'd mistaken our fourth floor flat with the attic where occasionally, in really bad weather, a homeless person would find shelter. I gave him a little money, and guided him upstairs.
It was fairly common practice.

"Come and look at this!" Helen shouted.

Our flat was also next door to the then world famous sadist club, the "Club de Sade", where a client had obviously tried to leave without paying. There he was, in the middle of the street on a quiet Sunday afternoon, being chased up and down by four leather clad beauties, (black leather bodices, thigh length boots, leather masks, the whole shebang), who were knocking the living daylights out of him with bullwhips. He had a huge smile on his face, and my guess is that later, he was billed twice. We suddenly recognized one of the girls as our next door neighbour, who often came and had Sunday dinner with us. She tried to explain to us over our next meal together that she wasn't in fact a prostitute, no sex, but having a good hiding was quite permissible. Weird!

For a while, I took over running the bar next door, working during the day on site, and working nights in the bar, with Helen doing the day shift. Often, the working girls would come in and ask if they could run their businesses from the Bar, but I always refused, not so much on moral grounds, mainly because I was quite fond of my kneecaps.

116

I had been warned!

We tried to turn it into an English pub atmosphere with a darts board and pool table and it was doing quite well as we were the only place to serve up English breakfasts on a Sunday morning in Hamburg, which coincided with people heading home from the all night sessions at the fish market.

We once did eighty breakfasts in a morning which meant Helen was getting remarkably fit, carrying each order down what we later worked out were ninety two steps, but we quickly realized it was killing us and enough was enough.

We eventually gave the bar up, as the strain was beginning to tell. We were starting to argue and fall out in a big way, mainly because we were working ourselves to a frazzle.

But, it has to be said, I maintain to this day that this was still one of the happiest years of our marriage.

Hamburg was a place I'd always wanted to visit, having read about the Beatles living there in the early sixties, and the Reeperbahn, considering it was one of the biggest sex areas in Europe, felt a remarkably safe place to be. It was so heavily policed. We remained here for almost a year, and it was, looking back, a wonderful time and a good start to married life.

Our local bar was the Seaman's Mission, where the Beatles had stayed in their time in Hamburg. Helen and I had our first Xmas dinner together here. I'd pop in every night on the way home, where we drank a few beers and played pool with many different peoples, including a whole bunch of West Africans, who occasionally lost it, usually with each other, and the guns would appear. It was usually time to throw the game.

117

A fond memory of Hamburg is courtesy of the British Navy.

They'd sent a ship over, H.M.S. Intrepid, for the three hundredth birthday of Hamburg, and Dougie, Helen and I, as guests of a couple of Petty Officers we'd met in the Seaman's Mission, and became friendly with while they were in port, watched an amazing fireworks display from the rear deck, suitable refreshed with English Beer from the mess.

The Navy did us proud.

The English lads would continue to misbehave, especially Andy from Leeds, who blew his very large pay packet on the first night. This was today's equivalent of at least eight hundred pounds, and we later heard at least three hookers were involved. He then slept the night away in a bus shelter, because he didn't have the bus fare back to the hotel.

But time was moving on and it was time for a change of scenery. We had had a good year here, lived well, loved well, and saved little, but had a memorable first year. It was time for a new adventure, and South Africa beckoned.

We had a lovely, day today

<u>Day fourteen – Monday 9th July 2007.</u>

Myrian phoned at one O'clock this morning from Texas. Not
the D.I.Y. store, the other Texas, where George W, the saviour
of the free World, and his dad, old George, live. The one in the
good old US of A.

Myrian is my eldest, younger sister. She'd got the time
difference all mixed up.

Despite the interrupted sleep, I woke up in fine spirits and
went for an hours "Crutching", round the village, which turned
into an all morning activity. I swear, if I ever move into a new
town, or village, the first thing I'll do is buy a pair of crutches,
and wander around for a week.
It sort of opens people up.

This time I got a bit more organized and wore cycling gloves
because the hands haven't hardened up yet, and I took an MP3
player to listen to.
Then

I returned home, and waited for an email from "The McCourts
of New York", Frank McCourt, and the family.

Well, ok, not quite, but I'd had an idea, and started following a
thread!
You see, Bob really had given me a lift yesterday where
writing the book was concerned, and so last night, while Helen
was out at Church, I started looking into how to publish a
book. All the while I'm writing this, I'm thinking that I hope
the kids enjoy it and how much it's keeping my mind focused
and to be honest, how much I'm enjoying doing it.
Publishing seems all of a sudden very serious. But why not
look into it? I haven't a lot to lose, and besides, Bob seems to
know what he's talking about.

119

The internet seemed a good place to start and I eventually ordered a book on how to find a literary agent. It seemed a good place to start.

The thought then crossed my mind. "Who do I know who has done this sort of thing before?"

And the answer was of course, "Nobody".

So I thought, "I'll see how the other McCourts did it ", and started doing some research on the internet. I couldn't find Frank McCourt's website, but did find his brother Malachy's.

I then discovered that Malachy has a son, Malachy junior, who coincidently enough, is a Diving Instructor, in Bali, and had trained to be a diver, in Thailand, just like my boy Andrew. When I discovered my Venezuelan family, the coincidences there were amazing. Or is it that I have a very shallow gene pool which doesn't need a lifeguard.

I took a chance, and I emailed Malachy junior, explaining the reason for writing the book, *and to see if there were any jobs for The Boy for next season.*

A little cheeky, but you never know.

Malachy junior replied that he would happily pass on anything I send him to his dad…happy days. As you can imagine, it's given me a bit of a boost, and so I'm waiting patiently for an email from the famous man himself….or not as the case might be.

Anyhow, this is the interesting bit…

I then thought, "What if he does get in contact and he asks, where our branch of the family came from?" You can see the thread I'm following, yes?

I haven't a clue, *and right now, all of a sudden, it seems important to me to find out just exactly where I've come from, but more to the point, I didn't want to look stupid!*

I've spent the past week or so looking back at my life, so why not look back a little further in time to see where I've really come from. How much of who I am today is really a result of my life's experiences, and how much has come down from previous generations? How much is environmental and how much is Genetic? I have absolutely no idea.

So I phoned up my Uncle Vic and asked him where his grandfather, my great grandfather came from? His reply was,

" About three hundred yards down the road."

He had no idea either, but I'd awakened his interest and he went off to see what he could find out.

This old family tree thing was starting to excite me. I'd been watching ,"Who do you think you are?" on the TV, and thought it would be nice to actually discover long lost ancestors and find out just where I did come from. I only knew about the family history as far back as my Great Grandmother, and that was it. Where we came from was a total mystery to me, and whether it's all to do with the emotions I am experiencing at the moment, finding out where it is I've come from, and more importantly, who it is I've descended from has taken on some importance.

It should be interesting.

At the moment, I'm in the doldrums!

Where the cancer is concerned, it's a treading water sort of time, a nothing happening time where everything seems so normal. Helen hasn't thrown a healthy yoghurt at me for four days now and has gone back to work.

The phone has stopped ringing, and I'm losing all sense of time.

These are indications we're still in Phase two.

I still get the daily lunchtime phone call from Laura. Claire and Andrew have just popped in to read the latest ramblings.

Even the weather is boring, with a quick visit from summer in the mornings, only to watch it being washed away again by lunchtime.

As I said, it's all so normal, and time is beginning to drag.

So today, to preserve my sanity and give myself something to do, I spent a great deal of time looking up my McCourt family tree.

On my father's side, I already knew that Grandfather Rivero had been a Colonel in the Venezuelan Army. Myrian remembers him riding on a big white horse, carrying a big sword, but only knew that my Grandad had been born in the workhouse sometime around 1910.

I thought it was a good time to check out the McCourt pedigree.

Friendsreunited is a brilliant website.

My first visit was in 2002, when someone at school told me the story of how one of our female colleagues had been on the internet, and rediscovered her old boy friend through Friendsreunited, a website designed to find long lost friends. Some time later, so the tale went, her partner had walked in on them on the sofa, in front of the fire in, shall we say, an inappropriate state of undress, and apparently there was hell to pay! But that's not why I went on…..

This time I visited Genesreunited, a sister website, in an attempt to find out where we McCourts came from, and, by cheekily asking if I can look at the family trees of other members, have discovered hundreds of possible relations, from the Whitehaven area alone.

I sent emails, asking for the details of fourteen family trees in the Whitehaven area, to people who were registered as having name McCourt recorded somewhere, and my first positive reply came from a member, "Sue in 10b", who, bless her, sent me lots of information to help with my search. The trend does seem to be that the McCourts in Whitehaven can originally be traced back to leaving Ireland sometime around the 1800's.

I'm now waiting with excitement for more replies.

So, where did we go next.

Helen and I had decided to make a new life in South Africa. There was a lot of construction work going on down there and I'd contacted a German firm I'd previously worked for, who said to contact the company when I got to Jo'burg, but gave no real guarantees of employment. By the time we'd paid for the tickets, we had the grand total of about £80 left to start a new life. It was the start of another adventure.

We were due to fly out on "Air Zaire", on our first wedding anniversary, but after we'd spent four hours sitting about Heathrow Airport, we heard that our flight had been delayed, *for five days*.

Not the best of starts.

Most of the other passengers went back home, but around thirteen of us diehards kicked up hell, and refused to leave. Where we were concerned, we really had no choice. We just couldn't afford to go back home, and after a great deal of arguing, the airline representative finally agreed to put us up in a hotel, "The Heathrow Ambassador", until the plane was fixed.

He returned later in the evening to take us all out for a meal, on the airline, as an apology....his first mistake.

Now, this poor bloke had been topping himself up with wine or whatever he could drink on a flight back from Brussels, to pick up enough courage to give us the bad news, and by the time we had finished our meal, he was well and truly plastered....his second mistake.

We'd got friendly with Mark and Jill, a young couple like ourselves, who were off to spend a few months touring the country in a campervan, when the opportunity arose to invite the airline Rep back to Mark's room for a night cap, where, (after a polishing off the best part of a bottle of Brandy which we'd persuaded him to nick from the bar), he collapsed unconscious.
I looked at Mark, and Mark looked at me, and morning arrived with one confused airline representative waking up naked in the bath, more worried about where his expensive French undies were, than about the photos we'd pretended to have taken.

124

I sort of added to the story by acting camp, and telling him I'd got in the bath with him. He went a light shade of pale....

Eventually, we gave him his clothes back, and off he went home to change. To his credit, he returned at lunch time, looked at Mark and myself, and announced that the airline had agreed to foot the bill for whatever we ordered, food, drink, the lot.

He turned out to be a brilliant bloke, and gave us a wry smile, when five days later, we told him we'd made the whole thing about the photos up.

We partied for five days, had a brilliant first wedding anniversary, courtesy of Air Zaire, and finally boarded the plane, with lots of new friends, more like a coach trip to Blackpool, than flying off to a new life inAfrica.

After a six hour stop over in Zaire, most of it spent sitting on the runway with our luggage, we landed in Johannesburg at teatime, on a Friday, with a meager £40 left in the kitty, and a quick phone call to the German Company I'd worked for in Europe resulted in an interview for the Monday morning, with the view to traveling out to work on a construction site, out into the bush on the Tuesday, all being well.

Which left us to find somewhere for the weekend.

A bus took us to the Centre, and a taxi to a bar in Hillbrow where we had a beer and said goodbye to Mark and Jill, agreeing to keep in touch. A few weeks later, we met up again, and had our first Xmas in South Africa with them, and their wonderful Rhodesian family up in the Magaliesburg mountains. It was simply the best Xmas I'd ever had.

After walking for about thirty minutes, we found ourselves outside a hotel in a seedy suburb of Johannesburg, not knowing the reputation the area had of being somewhat dangerous after dark.

I left Helen outside with the suitcases, while I went in to look for a room. I walked into the bar, and standing there was Davy. Pure coincidence!

Davy was a bloke I knew from my time in Rotterdam, ex SAS, and the foreman for a gang of welders who were down from Secunda, where I hoped to be the following week. At the time, Secunda was the biggest single construction site in the world and about a three hour drive out into the sticks.

Davy was a legend in the Industry, and the story goes that he had once swum out to an oil rig in the North Sea, on an airbed, pretending to have been washed out from the beach, returning with his SAS buddies a few days later and taking it over as part of a security operation.

I checked at reception, and they told me that all the rooms were full. I returned to the bar and mentioned it to Davy. (Did I mention Davy's glass eye. He'd have made a brilliant pirate!)

"Leave it to me ", he said, and off he went to have a word with the manager. This apparently involved Davy gently massaging the manager's throat against a wall, however he returned with a smile on his face, "it's all sorted". What a man!

I went and found Helen, who was feeling quite at home, having been propositioned twice already, and in that short time, had actually found us a Christian commune to stay in, simply by asking a passing African lady. What was this apartheid we'd heard so much about?

We decided to have the weekend in the hotel, move into the commune on the Sunday, and so the party continued for the weekend. Construction lads look after each other, and I don't think we paid for a drink the whole weekend.

I had the interview on the Monday morning, and went up to Secunda the following day leaving Helen in Jo'burg while I sorted somewhere for us to live. I came back on the following Friday for the weekend, and off we went back up to the site the following week.

All my instincts said that coming to South Africa was a good idea. That first weekend in Johannesburg, I gave away our return airline tickets to somebody in the hotel who needed them. I'd decided we were here to stay and there was no going back.

My five years in South Africa were simply the best years of my life.

I worked harder and longer during my time here, and learned more about life during this period than at any other. My girls were both born here, and I had success.

In Secunda, I worked as a Construction Site Foreman on the Oil from Coal Construction site, at the time, the world's biggest. We lived on a farm complex, which consisted mainly of prefabricated housing, next to an African village, about fifteen miles from the nearest town, Secunda, The place was the nearest thing to the wild west I've ever come across, thirty thousand construction workers on site, and one hotel, The Holiday Inn. (At the time it was reputed to have been the fastest turning over Holiday Inn in the world.) It was never less than six deep at the bar.

Helen and I moved into an old caravan, on the farm, with a view of the stars. Actually it was a hole in the roof, which we fixed up, and turned into a very cosy home from home, which meant we could live for free, and save all our earnings, to get a good start in a new country. Fortunately for us, there were also another English couple on site, Meg and Brian Dover, with Helen and Meg the only two women on a farm of about twenty contracting men. Meg was camp cook, and dinner was always superb, ready and on the table, at the end of each working day.

My best mate was John Cullinan, who was descended from the chap who found the Star of Africa, in the Crown Jewels. He was Rhodesian who'd had enough of the troubles in his home country, and had literally packed everything he owned into his car, and drove over the border to start a new life in South Africa. He was the coolest dude I've ever met.

A couple of years later, John turned up at our house with the customary six pack and bottle of wine and nonchalantly asked if him and his new wife, Louise, could stay over for a few days. "Not a problem mate, why what's up?" I ask.

"The house had burned down!", replies John,

I thought he was joking, and it was later, actually about two beers later, when I heard Louise crying in the living room that I realized he was actually serious.

But for a new couple starting out in a new Country, it was brilliant. In the situation we were in, it was the best start we could hope for. We spent time together, had amazing African sunrises and sunsets, and above all else, I learned the art of barbequing, mainly from John.
Helen and Meg became firm friends and supported each other, leaving me to work all the hours available to put money away for whatever came next.

Whatever came next was Laura.

Not straight away you understand, but five weeks after landing in Jo'burg, Helen dropped the bombshell she was pregnant.

I was over the moon.

By the time Laura was born, we'd sorted an apartment down in Johannesburg, furnished top to bottom with everything brand spanking new, nursery included. I learned to focus on working for what I wanted, and this stayed with me forever. After six months on site, Helen moved back to Jo'burg while I went to work on other contracts, initially in Newcastle, then down to Zululand to open up the Richard's Bay area for the company.

Laura was born 11th October 1982, in Johannesburg, a day I'll never forget. Just after the birth, I popped over to the Hotel across from the Hospital for a celebratory beer. Looking up, I saw about twenty very beautiful girls coming down the staircase, and later found out they were this years "Miss South Africa" contestants.

I didn't look twice at them, I'd already seen the most beautiful girl in the world, at 8.17.a.m. that morning.

The following day I was sent back to Secunda, newly promoted as Site Manager, which meant leaving Helen alone, with Laura, in hospital for the next week. The opportunity to run my own project had appeared, I couldn't turn it down. Looking back, it wasn't fair, and I regretted leaving them both, but an opportunity like this was what I'd been waiting for. But Helen is nothing if not tough and resilient, qualities I have always respected in her.

Two weeks later, she went home to Mum.

Six weeks later, she returned, and we moved up to the farm, together at last as a family. I loved South Africa. I loved the climate, I loved the proud African people, I loved the sunsets, the sunrises, and the amazing star filled Skies. I thought we'd be here for life!

Looking back, South Africa was something of a challenge. Sometime, during the five years I spent in this extraordinarily beautiful country, I became a man. It was a time where I went through a full spectrum of emotions, from the success of real achievement to the depression of almost losing everything that was ever important to me.

It was still the best time of my life.

A mere nine months after landing in the Country, as a cowboy, and working on the tools, I was back in Secunda as a Site Manager on a small project. It was that sort of place. I was now in charge of a crew of fifty men, with the responsibility of a million rand project. It couldn't have happened anywhere else in the world, and I was loving it. I thrived on it, and realized that not only was I enjoying what I was doing, I was actually good at it. My confidence soared.

We were three young couples out on the farm, Stuart, my sheet metal worker foreman and Carol, his partner, and their baby Stuart, as well as another couple who rented a mobile home from the company, Phil and Irene. We three men would go to work early every day, each coming home to a loving wife every night. My added bonus was that I also came home to a lovely gorgeous baby girl to love and cherish. The money was great, and the job was going well. Helen, Laura and I had the flat in Johannesburg to go home to every alternate weekend, to get a bit of city life, while out on the farm, we still lived in the old caravan, looking much better thanks to Helen, but the old caravan nevertheless, and everything was blissful in the McCourt household.

Occasionally, the workload meant that we needed additional people to work with us, and it was here that I met Steve, the unluckiest bloke I'd ever met.

Steve was a Brummie, and had come over to South Africa, on the off chance that he could get some work in Insulation. When he'd landed, he went directly to his brother's place, thinking he could stay here until something turned up.

His brother opened the door, saw it was Steve, and promptly closed it again.

His brother had a reputation amongst the lads as a total bastard, so when Steve told us the story, nobody was really very surprised. Steve was sent up to us from Head Office at a time when we were particularly short of supervisors and the first words I heard from him, on the Monday morning, his first day at work were, "Sorry I'm late mate. Puncture!" this, his first day on the job.

On his way to the site, he'd picked up a flat tyre on the dirt roads. It happens, no big deal, the day passed, and Steve came back to the farm where he would spend the week with us.

Unfortunately, Steve's bad luck was only just beginning.

We set off together in a little convoy, early the following morning, and amazingly, Steve arrived two hours later than the rest of us, his word being, "Sorry I'm late again mate. Puncture!"

Well, coincidences do happen.

So you can imaging my surprise when the following day when Steve, this time only one hour late behind us, finally turned up after having yet another puncture. This in itself wasn't yet something to dwell on, but what he'd done was panic, after the stick we'd given him the previous day. He'd left the van where it was, got a lift off another vehicle to the main gate where he'd then ran in through the security checkpoint, without checking in.

This was the same site that had been under a rocket attack three weeks before I first started working here, and security was something that the South Africans took incredibly serious. They tend to shoot you!

Security turned up looking for him, after discovering the abandoned vehicle, inside the security perimeter, by which time, he'd run off again, to go back and fix the puncture, and I wasted the rest of the morning appeasing some very angry looking South African policemen, carrying automatic weapons.

The following day, we decided to have a barbeque.

We'd all decided to go to the butchers to get some meat, along the lines of me the steak, Stuart the sausages, Phil the burgers, and it was left to Steve to get the Chicken. He turned up, yet again, two hours late, with three big drums of Colonel Sanders, Kentucky fried best. *He'd had another puncture*, missed the butchers, panicked, and drove miles to the nearest fast food outlet to get the chicken. He was starting to get a reputation.

Later in the evening, when we'd all had a few drinks, I asked Steve about his brother.

"He's a bastard and I hate him!", was Steve's reply, and he spent the rest of the evening very pissed at the way the week had gone, and at the way his brother had treated him when he'd first arrived in the Country.

The following day, I got a phone call from my boss, Garry.

"Can you give Steve some bad news Billy?".

"Sure," I reply, convinced that I was going to have to tell him he'd been sacked.

"Can you tell him his brothers dead! "

I was stunned. We'd only just spent the night discussing what a bastard the bloke was, and this appears out of nowhere. Apparently, the brother had had the great idea to rob a security van down in Durban where he was working. He'd taken along a replica pistol, but hadn't known that the South African police had gotten wind of his little escapade. In the back of the Security van sat an armed police marksman who had opened fire the second the door had opened.

Despite what he'd said the night before, he was still his brother, and Steve was devastated. He had the unsavory job of flying down to Durban to identify the body, where the police had taken great satisfaction in telling Steve that his brother had taken forty six minutes to die.

They'd also left the body with his hands, with bullet holes through the middle of each palm, up in front of his chest, with the eyes wide open.

They were making a point.

Steve cracked up. In a short space of time, he flew back to England, leaving South Africa for good. I was soon to realize that South Africa could also be an unforgiving place, and wasn't always quite the paradise it seemed.

Time passed, and I went from strength to strength, next having a job as assistant site superintendent on a large pulp mill project, out in the bush at a place called N'godwana, more commonly called n' godforsaken. Actually, it was a beautiful place, and the company had put me up in a resort at Sudwala, where I could open my front door, and dive straight into a lovely swimming pool. I could wake up, jog, swim, have breakfast, and start the working day better than at any time in my life. It felt like I was living the dream. Helen had by now gotten a job at the British Consulate in Johannesburg, running the information department. This meant for weeks on end, I had to live away from home, but that was what contract work was all about, and was a way of saving money towards the time when I would be able to start up a business of my own.

"The Lion King", was a great kid's movie, and I love the soundtrack, "The Circle of Life". It's all about Africa, and always reminds me of Gerry, another mate.

I sometimes wonder even today if he's still wanted for murder?

Gerry was wanted for Murder in what is now called Zimbabwe, although it was then Rhodesia. As a younger man, or so the story goes, he'd gotten into a fight with a native Rhodesian, in a car park, where the man had died. To avoid extradition, Gerry jumped over the border into South Africa where he could begin a new life. A new job, a new wife, and a new family, a completely new beginning, only things tend to never be quite that simple...

134

Years before, Gerry had had a previous marriage, and a sixteen year old son who had grown up in England. Gerry had settled himself down in Richards Bay, a growing town on the Natal Coast, in Zululand, and somewhere along the line, the decision had been made for Gerry's son to come out from England, and join his father in a new life, together with his new family.

"I need a favour mate", asks Gerry on the phone one day.

By this time, I was back working at head office in Johannesburg, so Gerry continued,

" Can you pick my boy up from the airport for me this Wednesday?"

"Sure, no problem", I reply, giving him time to come up from the coast, and collect him at the weekend.

A few months later, Gerry's son manages to get an apprenticeship with the same company that Gerry was with, and everything in the garden looked rosy. He'd bought him a trials bike, and the lad would go off at weekend, riding along the many, many miles of sand dune by the Indian Ocean, that is abundant in that part of the world. He'd found himself a girlfriend,
He had a future and things couldn't get better….

A few weeks later, I get another phone call, from my mate Garry, the bearer of bad tidings.

"It's Gerry's lad…….He's been killed!".

My immediate thoughts turn to the trials bike thinking he'd been involved in some sort of motor accident, but not so. He'd gone out for a beer into a local hotel where he'd gotten into an argument with some Afrikaans lads, and sometime later that night, they'd followed him out into the Hotel car park, where they'd beaten him to death.

I got to thinking. I'd heard somewhere that there was a thirty million to one chance of being murdered. But twice…and in the same family….what were the chances of that happening?

And was the old saying true?

"The sins of the fathers…..were they passed down to the sons?"

Did, in some strange cosmic way, Gerry's lad pay the price of what his father had done those many years before?

I got to thinking that the world can be a cruel and bizarre place.

Moving on….
The next two or so years, in many ways, were probably the best two years of my life., but I'm not so sure. In some ways, they most certainly weren't.

I had eventually saved enough money to start the business, S and M Insulation, nothing to do with sado-masochism, but there were times I'd beat myself up if things didn't go the way it was intended.

No, it was simply the initials of our surnames.

In the early days, to get the business started, I'd spend hours walking around industrial estates around Johannesburg, handing out business cards, and knocking on doors. It didn't take me long to realize that it was much easier on the phone, and very slowly, we began to pick up work.

I'd bought tools and machinery and other equipment over the past two or so years, and with Stuart's old campervan, we put it all in a garage, called it our workshop, and off we went, with more enthusiasm than any real business sense, but I sort of hoped I'd pick this up on the way.

The timing just felt right.

Many of the bigger companies were downsizing in South Africa, and opportunities were opening up. With Stuart's amazing sheet metal working skills, and with what I'd learned running projects over the last couple of years, how could we fail?

By the end of the first year, we had moved into a proper workshop near to where we lived, had built up a regular crew of about twelve experienced African workers, who had been made redundant by the bigger companies, and here we were really fortunate to acquire the services of two really top Zulu foremen. I have to say that of all the peoples I have met around the world, the Zulu people I met were the most inspirational. I often recall with fondness the strength and dignity I witnessed on a daily basis from these guys, They were just great! I made sure we paid the best wages around, and I still believe to this day we had a workforce second to none.

The business started taking off.

The workforce got bigger and the jobs got bigger, and suddenly we were starting to make serious money. Stuart looked after the fabrication side of things while I did everything else. I'd be in the office at six, and often didn't get home until late at night but I was successful and was starting to overlook some of the more important things in my life.

And about this time, Helen became pregnant again.

She had by this time, a job at the British Consulate in Johannesburg and our social life started to blossom as well. We met a great deal of nice people through her work, and life was good. It was an endless round of parties, restaurants, and money wasn't a problem. By the time Claire was born on the 22nd August, 1985, we were making a good living. We had now forty two workers and things didn't look like they could get any better.

We decided to throw a party to celebrate a big cheque that had come in that week, and just as things were starting to liven up, Helen did the usual, "I think my waters have broken" thing that women do. We shot off to Jo'burg General, where Helen was taken into the delivery room while I looked after the paperwork. Exactly eleven minutes later, I caught up with the proceedings, only to find a head appearing from between Helen's legs.

Our Claire had decided to make an early appearance, and I can honestly say it's the last time she has turned up early for anything since. I remember looking down at her and saw the twinkliest and mischievous eyes imaginable, and knew straight away that our lives would never be the same again. She was gorgeous…a really bonny baby.

I had everything I'd wanted. The work was still coming in, as was the money, but something was wrong and the cracks were beginning to show. Our lives were changing in a way that didn't feel right, and it was difficult to slow down, and take stock. Stuart's relationship was a constant turmoil, and his partner would often leave him for months on end leaving the poor man in a very low way. It was difficult for him to deal with and the strain was beginning to tell.

Towards the end of that year, work started to slow down, and the business was having problems with getting money in. A big company had gone bust on us, owing us a great deal of money, but we could do little. It was a major setback, not the end of the world, but had happened at the wrong time. Coupled to the fact that I now had two daughters to look after, and the realization that we'd been away from England for over five years, resulted in what was a serious case of homesickness.

Helen had started to miss the family badly and we decided to return to England for Xmas. For the weeks leading up to our departure, I'd sit by the pool and watch the planes come in from England in the morning, and leave for England in the evening, and I knew it was time to make a change. South Africa was changing and deep down, I had the idea that I wanted the children brought up around family, in a country with good schools and a better health service.

Boy, was I wrong.

That Xmas, we made the decision to come back to England and start again, and to begin with I'd take a job working for Helen's dad until I found something better. Given the way the kids have turned out, and the good things we have in our lives today, maybe it was the right decision to make but if I'd realized then just how hard the next ten years were going to be, I can honestly say I would never have come back to England.

After the Xmas vacation, I went back to South Africa for two weeks only, by which time Stuart had cracked up and decided he'd also had enough. We virtually gave away everything we'd worked for in just two weeks, and Stuart headed off to the coast to work for a mate of ours. I jumped on a plane back to Blighty and life suddenly became hard.

I suppose over time I've tended to romanticize the whole South Africa experience because it was a time of my life when I really felt that I was truly successful, and maybe I have often tended to overlook the difficult times we faced. The major benefit of the whole experience was that, by the time we got back to England, the relationship that I now had with Helen was as solid as it could ever be. For five years we'd taken on the world and hadn't done a bad job of it, and we still have that with us today.

I've enjoyed reminiscing about this period in my life. It doesn't do any harm to look back and see where we did things right, or wrong. I suppose it's taken me back to a time where I battled hard and won, and there's no reason not to do it again. It could be an omen...

From my mother in law this morning :-
Five tips for a woman.
1. It is important that a man helps you round the house.
2. It is important that a man makes you laugh.
3. It is important to find a man you can count on and doesn't lie to you.
4. It is important that a man loves you and spoils you.
5. It is important that these four men don't know each other.

She is a little sweety! (No, not sweaty...aren't spellcheckers funny... in mean sweety!)

I was awake at Five this morning, fairly buzzing with excitement, because at around ten thirty last night, I received an email from Lisa, a long lost relative, who, along with her father Brian, had traced part of the McCourt family tree as far back as *the Seventeen Hundreds*. Gaps in the family jigsaw were being filled in, and she also told me that he had traced my grandfather's mother's lineage back to the 1600's, to a village in Yorkshire named Bentham. The records at the church in Bentham stopped about then, having been destroyed because of the Plague.

I'm reeling from the knowledge that I have Yorkshire blood in me....why me? I've lived here most of my life, but to have the stuff flowing through my veins? I'd better put a padlock on my wallet.
I'm still waiting for information on the McCourt lineage. I've cast the bread on the water, so let's see what bites! It's looking possible that if the famous McCourts ever do ask the question about where the family comes from, I may just have the answer.

My grandad's name was John McCourt, his father was John McCourt, his grandfather was John McCourt, and given the proliferation of John McCourt's in the Whitehaven area, it now explains why he was referred to as "Jack" all his life.

What I'm discovering is that writing this book is taking me on a journey into the past in more ways than one, which is in a very different direction to where I thought it would go, and not at all what I envisaged two weeks ago. I'm not only looking at my own personal history, but a little into the history of people who have gone before me. I suppose it's a comforting experience to find out where the gene pool began..

It's like the Cancer diary bit has taken a back seat for the time being while I go off and have my own episode of "Who do you think you are?"

The added bonus is that the people I've been meeting are really nice people, and a website like Genesreunited would probably make a good dating agency, given that I'm meeting people with similar interests. The only problem being is its maybe a bit too much like *"Deliverance"*, where you could end up dating your long lost cousin. I could be wrong, but I don't believe we've got a banjo player in the family yet.

But it is enjoyable, and it's got me thinking.

In a family tree, each of these people are simply a name in a little rectangular box linked to others, a network of who begat who so to speak.

In my family tree, I will be logged in my little rectangular box as," William McCourt b 1955.....,died... and that's it.

It's not a lot is it? Not Billy, but "William McCourt b 1955...

It's downright depressing.

Not Billy, the person, the life . Not ME the person! It somehow doesn't seem right, but such is the transience of life I suppose.

It's all a bit morbid isn't it? But as I've said, there are good days and there are bad days.

I suppose the pressure is building a little. Time is pressing on and it's nearly time to be thinking about my visit to Birmingham, What's more, Andy went back to Greece today. I drove him to Manchester Airport, stopping off at Laura's for a lovely meal. I know he's much more settled than when he arrived, because he slept most of the way there in the car.

In the week he has been back, he has safely moved from Phase one into Phase two. He's over the shock, and has moved into the acceptance phase.

He spent the last couple of nights at Claire's place, and is much more settled than when he arrived. I'm strangely glad he's going back to the job he loves doing, but I will miss him. I'll email him the ramblings daily so he can see how things are progressing.

Who knows, he might be in Bali by Xmas!

But I'd had enough. The family tree business was making me miserable and for days now, I'd been sitting by the phone, waiting for it to ring. I needed some time on my own.

It's not that I'm ungrateful for all the good wishes I've been receiving over the past couple of weeks, but this is something I've done all my life, taken off, sometimes on my bike, for three or four days at a time, to put things into perspective and get rid of the demons.

Saying goodbye to Andrew had made me miserable, and I'd gotten really, really fed up waiting for the phone call telling me when I'd be going into hospital. I came home, put the Television on, and saw that we were 1-0 up in the European under 21s, semi-final against the Dutch, and decided impulsively to jump into my campervan and drive to Hull, to get the ferry to Holland to watch the Euro U21's Final in the forlorn hope that England would win.

Some things never change, do they?

We never get to Soccer Finals because we always lose on penalties, don't we? This time we lost the semi-final on penalties to the Dutch! Once again, I'm disappointed to find out that we still can't win a match on penalties, although this time, we scored about thirteen… and we still didn't win!

To make it worse, I watched it in the lounge, on the North Sea Ferry, in Hull, and the boat hadn't even left the dockside.

I sort of felt despondent, but I just need some time to myself, surrounded by strangers who have no idea that I'm sitting here at the bar with a really serious illness. I need some normality right now, some denial I suppose, and maybe pretend a little that there really is nothing wrong with me. Who knows when or even if I will be able to do this again.

It's wasn't about the football really.

It was about getting my head together and preparing myself as best I could, for what's coming up next week.

<u>Day Seventeen – Thursday 12th July 2007.</u>

The phone rang at home this morning. Helen answered the phone.

"Mr McCourt?"

"No, it's his wife." Helen answered

"It's the Orthopedic Hospital. We've booked his operation for sometime next week. We'd like to have him down here on Sunday, so ……..".

Helen immediately got on the phone and gave me the bad news, and told me to come straight back home.

Phase Three has begun!
I finally got to Groningen in Holland, thinking I would get a ticket for the game, and shout for the Dutch in the Final, but it never happened. The Hospital in Birmingham had said could I be there first thing Monday morning, preferably Sunday afternoon and all I could do was turn the van round and come home.

The whole week got off to a fairly piss poor start all round.

Serves me right I suppose.
And I was starting to panic a little. I've got about four days left, and I'm being bombarded with some very illogical thoughts.

My first thought was, *"I haven't enough time to finish my book!"* It's an Alec Guinness moment from "Bridge over the River Kwai".

"I haven't finished with the diet", I've only lost ten pounds.

"I haven't finished my crutching!". I thought my chest and shoulders would be much, much bigger.

"It's too early...", the voice in my head was yelling.

I rang back to let Helen know I'd changed my ferry ticket and she kicked into gear, giving me instructions to ring the hospital... she's already started worrying about aftercare procedures.

S*he's been in Phase three for a while now!*

I'm having a lot of mixed feelings right now! On the one hand, I'm relieved that it's come round so quickly, and that by sometime next week, my Cancer will have been removed, which has got to be a good thing, right?

But on the other hand, there's a long operation, and a long recovery to go through, and of course the dreaded bowel movement thing. Then again, I will be unconscious, and won't know anything about it, so nothing to worry about there, and of course there are any amount of drugs available for immediately after, so the pain aspect is fairly under control. Everyone I've spoken to has told me how brilliant Morphine is...

As to recovery, and the future functioning of the man bits, I suppose I'll just have to be optimistic. I'm still worried about bedpans...all I can think of is please, please, please....just please let it not be a male nurse.... or even a hairy female one!

Helen's next phone call was to her Mum, which is code for putting it on the grapevine.

And the phone, this time my mobile phone, has started ringing again. Non-stop ringing again.

I drove four hours to the ferry terminal, and sat around in the terminal for another three hours. I'd always enjoyed ferry trips, but wasn't enjoying this one, and with what I'd got to look forward to, it was a long way home.

Mind you, it was always going to be a long ride home. No doubt, if we'd actually got to the final, we'd have been beaten on penalties.

<u>Day Eighteen – Friday, July 13th 2007. O Day minus three and counting.</u>

Text from Claire:-
"Liverpool Airport was shut down yesterday for eight hours, due to "a suspicious car".
Apparently, it had Road Tax, Insurance, and the Radio was still in it! ".

I got back home from Holland this morning and realized that my little jaunt was just a waste of time really. But I needed the time to just be on my own.

I needed it.

Today, my mind is flying off in all sorts of directions, and what is clear is that I'm not going to finish this book by the time I go to Birmingham.

There's simply not enough time.

I know in the bigger scheme of things, it's not all that important.

My original idea of keeping a log up to the day of the operation had a definite finality to it, which has been good for me on many levels, but once I'd started, I'd become less comfortable with this idea. It felt that my story would end with the operation, curtain falling, so to speak, but that's wrong. Besides, I hadn't realized how much I'd become immersed in my writing. Doing this has been great for me.
The focus should really be that simply getting back to a normal life, *beginning with the operation.*

Its about being positive .It makes far more sense if my operation is the mid-point, with a happy ending to follow, doesn't it?

And, if my aim in doing this book, that of reassuring my friends and family, and anyone else in a similar position, it to succeed, then it makes more sense to carry on.

Through the operation, into recovery, and beyond, so to speak.

I'm in a reflective mood today, and, as I've said, feel stupid for going off to Holland on a whim and wasting both time and money on what have been two wasted days.

The only thing I can do is be philosophical about the whole thing, and to be honest, it's the last of my worries.

So, moving on....

I spoke my cousin Janet today, amongst many others would had picked up the mother-in-laws smoke signals and I sort of dropped myself in it when I did the "Deliverance" and the "banjo playing" bit, about dating long lost cousins, forgetting that both herself, and her husband of the past twenty seven years, my half cousin John, are both little acorns on the family tree. A tense moment, but fortunately, she did see the funny side.

I mentioned that I'd had the great idea about writing a book, and told her I'd been up to mischief in trying to get in touch with the other famous McCourts about maybe getting it published.

She thought I'd lost my marbles. Then our Janet said,

"Why don't you ask our Colin?".

149

"Why would I ask our Colin?"…..still "Our Colin", my cousin even though I'd only set eyes on him twice in the last thirty years, at, you've guessed it, a funeral.

"What does Colin know about writing books?"

I now know that Colin had a book published on the history of a slum area in Whitehaven, where many of the mining families lived, called "Newhouses".

He's a bloody author for goodness sake!

It's amazing what happens when we follow a thread. Another twist in the journey!

I phoned him up, and we had a brilliant chat about the old days. It turns out that Colin had, until recently, been working at the local Mining Museum, in Whitehaven, and has a passion for the history of the area. When I mentioned to him that I was interested in finding out about the family tree, I was astounded to find out that he had already done it, and had traced the lineage back to one *John McCourt 1784*, believed to be from Ireland.

We talked for ages about growing up in Whitehaven and of the history of the place, and I learned such a lot about the town where I grew up, stuff that I just didn't know about.

Some very strong memories came flooding back.

I wrote earlier that as a small boy I used to play with Eric Nicholson on the old Miners Welfare.

I had forgotten that Eric's father had been killed in a local pit disaster.

I have also just remembered a day at Infant School when the mine ambulance went racing past with alarm bells ringing, and I was convinced my Dad was hurt, or worse, killed down the pit. I cried all day, stopping only when I got home and saw him standing there.

And, when I mentioned this to my oldest mate, Terry, he quietly reminded me that it was a mining accident that had left his father unable to work for the rest of his life.

It was all around us.

This was, however, setting a few alarm bells ringing, because it was unsettling me, and it wasn't as if I wasn't unsettled enough today.

You see, I'd left Whitehaven many years ago, and although I have visited quite often, it was usually to do the shopping, when we were down at Wasdale in the caravan. It wasn't for any spiritual journey into nostalgia, and I now have to ask myself, did I want to emotionally go back to a place that held such unhappy memories? I realize that, to a certain extent, being raised in Whitehaven had affected greatly my formative years, and for this I should be grateful.

But many of my memories of growing up there don't exactly warm the cockles of my heart, as you've probably gathered.

As a young teenager, *I hated the place*, but I suppose it was more about the experiences I'd had there, and not really the place itself. Some places just don't seem to work for some people, and when I'd finally left the town for good, I'd been glad to see the back of it, and have since spent most of my life living in places that have worked better for me.
But it's the sort of place that just keeps pulling you back
...*and I still keep going back.*

I still, after all these years, enjoy walking around the town, looking at all the changes, and remembering some of the better times, because there were happy times.

And deep down, I suppose I've kept the hope alive for years that people would eventually change the way they behaved for the bette… but they never seem to…

I don't know how true this is, but a mate of mine once told me that the reason we keep going back to the places which have hurt us in some way, is to make it better, even though deep down inside, we know it's not going to happen.

Yet we still keep going back. We still keep trying…

The question in my mind I suppose is, *"Is it worth the hassle?"*

"Do I actually need to go to places which I'd left behind me years ago? I've got a brilliant life now, and live in a lovely part of the world.

"Why bother?"
But what came through today in an email from Colin has surprisingly changed my way of thinking a little. He emailed me the following information which sort of had the effect of making the family tree thing a bit more real.

The following are news reports concerning some earlier McCourts, from the local newspaper at the time.

NAME: James McCourt

ADDRESS: 26 Mid Street Kells

AGE: 36

JOB: Hewer   Lamp No 128

WORKPLACE: 6 North No 4 Cavill

FOUND: September 29th Thursday

STATUS: Married to Martha

CHILDREN: Five, Thomas 9, Twins Margaret and John aged 8, Robert 5 and Elizabeth aged 3

RELATIVES LOST: Brothers Robert and Thomas

CHURCH: Town Mission

BURIED: Wednesday October 5th, Whitehaven

I.D.BY: Thomas Mccourt, father

NAME: Robert McCourt

ADDRESS: 17 Mid Street Kells

AGE: 34

JOB: Hewer   Lamp No 28

WORKPLACE: 6 North 4 cavill

FOUND: September 29th Thursday and 6 North

STATUS: Married to Mary Agnes

CHILDREN: One, Elizabeth aged 4 months

I.D.BY: Thomas McCourt father 6 Mid street Kells

I.D: --------

RELATIONS LOST: Brothers James and Thomas

CHURCH: Town Mission

BURIED: Tuesday October 4th, Whitehaven

NAME: Thomas McCourt Jun

ADDRESS: 4 Mid Street, Kells

AGE: 29

JOB: Hewer   Lamp No 129

WORKPLACE: 6 North No 4 Cavill 6 Level

FOUND: September 29th, Thursday

STATUS: Married to Susanagh

CHILDREN: One, James aged 19 months

I.D.BY: Thomas McCourt father 6 Mid Street, Kells

I.D: --------

RELATIVES LOST: Brothers James and Robert

CHURCH: Town Mission

BURIED: October 5th, Whitehaven

OTHER INFORMATION: Thomas McCourts father of the 3
brothers was an old man and identifying them had been a
terrible ordeal. He told the coroner in tears, they were 3 fine
lads. The coroner was visably moved as he handed him the
three death certificates and offered his deepest sympathy.
After the funerals this notice was in the Whitehaven News:
Mr and Mrs McCourt desire to thank all friends for sympathy
shown them by officials and members of the Miners Union,
members and committee of Kells Reading Rooms, members of

West Cumbria Pigeon Flying Club and the Bearers, owing the loss of their 3 sons in The Wellington Pit Disaster.

This was from a write up reporting the deaths of men killed in the Wellington Pit Disaster of 1910 one of many pit disasters that had happened in the town.

These three brothers were members of my family tree, and just the act of reading this has opened up something inside me. Their cousin Thomas, grandad's uncle was also killed that day and it doesn't feel right to mention any more about my family tree without their inclusion.

In one brief moment in history, three McCourt women became widows, and seven McCourt children became orphans.

The family tree thread had just gotten a little more serious all of a sudden.

There are places in our past and events in history which are still a part of us today and no matter how we try, there's no denying the fact that they are there.

I had earlier mentioned, that miners were a proud people. For many years now, my Uncle Vic has consistently shown a strong passion for his mining past, in the way he has sent me commemorative gifts over the years as if to say,

"You might have left home a long time ago, but don't dare you forget who you are!"

It's only recently I've began to realize that, to some extent, the same pride in who we are and where we've come from applies to the descendants of Mining folk. The way that Colin, in his book, and in his research keeps the memories of these young

156

men alive is very touching. I now feel, that our family tree has a spiritual connection to those who went before us, and yes, although I've been away a long, long time, it's still very much a part of who I am today.

What is strange though, is that this is the first I have heard of this, and why wasn't I told earlier....?

I feel I should have known about this.... and feel a little guilty that I didn't..

Was it too painful an episode in History to remember....or was it simply that it happened so long ago and just isn't all that important today? Or am I having these feelings because the news that I'm having an operation next week has set my senses on fire? And once I'm over this temporary phase in life, will any of this still be important? I just don't know.

A big part of this journey is about now, and about me becoming the man I am today. What I'm finding out is that a family tree gives us a place in History. There are over two hundred years of mining in our family and a great deal of suffering has taken place and because of this, we're a tough breed, and have shown we can put up with hardships. I hope to take a great deal of strength from these recent, and long forgotton memories.

I can see clearly now why my Grandfather, after fifty two years as a miner, worked until seventy unloading fishing boats on the fish quay. It was about being outside in fresh air and sunshine, or maybe the alive feeling we sometimes have after being out walking in a storm. Experiences of just feeling alive, that would be of major importance to man, who'd spent a great deal of his life underground.

He was a tough man, my Dad was, who lived his life in a harsh world, and I can only hope I can take some of his grit with me to Birmingham to get me over the next few weeks and months. After all, it is in the genes...and I have a strong feeling that this little chapter in my life story is only beginning....

<u>Day Nineteen – Saturday 19th July 2007. O day minus two
and counting.</u>

I quite like the "minus two and counting bit" I've added, don't
you?
It's like Tom Hanks in Apollo Thirteen heading toward blast
off, giving the proceedings a feeling of tension and of a
journey into the unknown. My journey isn't into the unknown.

*It's along the A64, across the M62, then down the M6 to
Birmingham.*

Today is packing day. I'm making it up as I go along, but I
suppose shorts and t-shirts will be the dress code for the days
on the ward, but I'm also wondering if I'm going to be
spending a lot of time in one of those surgical gowns. If so, I'll
try and remember to put in on the right way this time,
apparently, at least in the X-ray department in Scarborough,
modern ones fasten at the front, and there's no need to hold the
back bits together with your hand to stop your bum from
showing.

And why didn't someone tell me earlier?

Helen moved into Phase three in a fairly predictable way.

*She decorated the downstairs toilet. She is now weeding the
garden in the rain.*

I guess she feels the need to keep busy.
It may have felt that I've done nothing but reminisce the last
few days, but I have been making my preparations, planning
better I hope, than the inept suicide bombers at Glasgow
Airport. I have a new toiletry bag, courtesy of my little mate
Marilyn, as Helen now refers to her mother, and how times
have changed.

I remember in the early days when I first stole the daughter away from the family bosom, the Mother in Law looked at me like she would a skid mark on a fluffy white hotel towel, and now she's my little mate.

Helen's made me buy new underwear because she reckoned my usual stuff was past it, a disgrace she says, why, I don't know, I mean, it's not as if anyone ever sees them. She said I should splash out on some new ones, but my guess is that if the operation isn't entirely successful, *I could be splashing out more than I realize…sorry, a bit tacky…couldn't resist it…*

I've also sorted out my entertainment package, for the next three to four weeks.

For the past twenty three weeks I've recorded the whole of series three of "Boston Legal". (Which I think is brilliant, and William Shatner's best work to date!)….I am devastated that the twenty fourth, and last episode is next Wednesday so I guess I'll have to watch it when I get home.
I have boxed sets of "Boston Legal" series one…. series four and five of "24"….series one of "House" (which I'll keep in reserve in case I get too cheerful)…. and series one to four of "Spooks".

I also have in my suitcase about a dozen films on DVD if this lot runs out.

I have also with me an MP3 player, over six hundred songs on my new Ipod, two audio books to listen to, six ordinary books to read, and of course, one extraordinary book to write, I'm hoping…and I'm hoping it's enough!

And I've just had an Internet message, from my little sister Irma.

It read," LOS QUIERO MUCHO!".

It means "we love you", but it's in Spanish and I don't speak much Spanish, and unfortunately, Irma, Soraya, Maibe, Iraida, and Hector, my other brother and sisters, don't speak much English.
Myrian and Luis Armando, the other brother and sister, and both younger than myself, do speak English, which helps enormously.

I'm their big brother!

I'll explain another time.
Today. it seems important to get all the little jobs done, like putting the campervan away for the summer.

"It smells of holidays!" cried Helen, a little disappointed because we'd planned to go to Italy next week.

We washed down my little boat and covered it up to protect it from nasty bird droppings, took the audio books back to the Library, and generally took care of the little jobs which seem to have taken on an importance and urgency they hadn't had previously.

The phone's been ringing with well wishers sending their best, but I'm ready, I really am. I've been over the operation at least a thousand times, in my mind, the long recovery time and what it entails, *and I am sound of mind, if not of body.*

The audio books seemed a good idea for the first few days when I may be too weak to hold and read a book.

Sarah and Megan, my nieces, came round in the afternoon with gifts, and DVDs for Helen to watch in Birmingham. I actually spent all afternoon trying to put some structure into

the writing I've done to date, and expect to be doing this
frequently in the near future, for it all to make sense.
I suppose I'm going to have to pack sometime, but I don't
think I'll be needing a dinner jacket, or dressing up clothes
where I'm going.

It's not like I'm off to Italy, worse luck.

Tonight we went to an Italian Restaurant though, with Carl
and Claire, carbo-loading for the big event. I wanted a really
hot curry to make sure all the plumbing is sorted out before we
leave, so to speak, the memory of the male nurse still haunts
me, but Helen has put her foot down.

The meal was superb, and the atmosphere really lovely, Claire
laughing throughout, a really lovely night. We went down to
the In-laws, and met up with Tim, Karen and family, for last
goodbyes and a few hugs. *I'm starting to get worried because
of the way everyone else is getting worried about me.*

I realize what a magic family I've married into, their support
of late, indeed all the way through has been amazing.

I've spoken more to my mother over the last week than at
anytime in the last year or so. I have honestly tried to be
forgiving, and the recent recollections of times gone by have
done a great deal to put where I am now in life, into
perspective.

You see, while I haven't made my millions, I have achieved a
level of wealth far in excess of anything money can buy,
namely Helen, Laura, Claire, Andrew, and a marvelous family,
and amazing friends. The last nineteen days has proven this
beyond any shadow of a doubt.

Tomorrow brings a new phase into my life, and I'm ready for it. I also need to come out the other end, safely and mended, so I can continue my ramblings into "part two" because I still have so much to add. I suppose that I've been arrogant assuming I could start from scratch, and write a complete book in just three weeks, but I've tried, and now that I've seen sense, a few more weeks is most welcome.

We're leaving early in the morning to pop in and see Laura for breakfast in Manchester, before traveling down to Birmingham for midday. I'm off to bed.

<u>Day Twenty- Sunday 20th July 2007. "O" day minus one and
counting.</u>

Driving over to Manchester, I spotted a dead badger by the
side of the road. Twenty miles further on, I saw another one.
Two dead badgers by the roadside in one morning, and don't
things come in threes?

I hope I see a third one soon!

Don't get me wrong. I like badgers. *In fact I am a Badger.*

It's true, and no, I may be a little stressed, but I haven't lost
the plot completely. I haven't time to explain now, so you'll
have to bear with me, *but I don't want to be the next "Badger"
to go the big badger Sett in the sky, so I hope I see another
one!*

Ok, not really, but today's the day that my imagination is just
running a little bit wild.

I am being visited by the "What if?" demons.

The day had started with gentle warm sunshine through the
bedroom window and Helen saying, "Can't we just stay in bed
all day? "

"What a good idea".
We popped into Laura's in Manchester on the way down to
Birmingham, for breakfast where we had big hugs and kisses,
amidst an atmosphere of calmness, and off we continued.

An hour or so later, we pulled into the car park of "The Royal
Orthopaedic Hospital, Birmingham", where it was raining cats
and dogs, and, this being St Swithins day, we are obviously in
for another few weeks of this appalling weather, but hey, what

164

should I care, seeing as I won't be coming out to play for a couple of weeks at least.

An hour later, I was standing outside getting soaked, transferring all of Helen's personal life support system into her room. She had decided long ago that this whole thing was something we were going through together, and she was moving into the Nurses hostel to be near me. To keep her sane, she had brought along her T.V., DVD player, CD player, digibox, radio, even some flowers and big fluffy cushions to really make herself at home for the next two or three weeks.

I checked in, and had the usual Blood Pressure and heart checks, as well as having my blood and weight looked at to make sure I was at my best for tomorrow's bout. I'd lost over seven pounds in less than three weeks, but in the back of my mind, I thought it was nowhere near enough. Still, too late now to change things.

But, as far as the ward staff were concerned, that was all they needed me for, so I could do what I liked for the rest of the day. It felt weird, sort of guilty like, sneaking out to the supermarket for a bite to eat, and some last minute stuff. So I hung around the ward for an hour or so when we returned, just in case I was needed for anything.

The guy in the next bed was an older chap, around seventy I would say, who'd had his leg amputated, and was in considerable discomfort. He was on some sort of gas which hissed gently on a regular basis, really quite quiet, but loud enough to stop me from reading. He was visited by a minister and together they prayed. I thought," I wonder why Jeff didn't come back to see me again?".

Then I met Happy Larry, the most miserable bugger I've ever met in my whole life. He was a lean looking guy in his fifties,

who was in for a check up or something or other, and, having had his operation, and having survived, thought he knew it all.......
He eyed me up like a Hyena would eye up his dinner and started with," I walked in here better than I walked out!".

Fairly normal thing to happen, seeing as he'd had his knee replaced, I thought, inwardly smiling and fairly happy with the way the day was going.

"Every Doctor I've ever seen said something different about infections", was his next move," They don't really know what will happen next you know."

"This is the only place in the country which will do operations like this, nowhere else will touch them!", he continued, not the "This is the best hospital in the Country for carrying out procedures like these", which is what I'd been telling myself for weeks. Miserable bugger.

I'd had enough and legged it over to Helen's room to be consoled, and kicking myself for not going to see the latest Harry Potter film which was showing down the road. We thought the risk of infection from others wasn't worth the risk. A little naïve really as it turned out.

But he'd started my imagination running again, and little things which I wouldn't think twice about were growing in size. The fact that I'd forgotten my slippers all of a sudden seemed important, but it wasn't as if I would be needing them all that soon, would it?

Helen walked back over to the ward with me much later, and at nine o'clock, after a big long cuddle, she left. Inside my head, a voice was yelling," Don't go, it's too early!" This was quickly followed by a, "Pull yourself together you wimp", and all the time trying not to show how nervous I was underneath the cool façade. In reality, tomorrow I would be asleep for most of the day, and Helen would be the one having to deal with things.

Laura, Claire and Carl are coming down for the day, visiting Cadbury world of Chocolate in fact, so it wouldn't be all downhill.

At about ten, I put my pyjamas on and got ready for bed.

"You're one of us now you're out of your day clothes", says Happy Larry. "You sort of resist it all day, but now you have just become a patient by the act of changing into pyjamas." Did I mention he was a miserable sod?

Maybe he's right though.

The rest of the night just dragged on. I couldn't get off to sleep properly, the bed seemed uncomfortable, and my mind was in a complete turmoil, making everything about tomorrow seem huge.

I've never had a big operation before? Ok, I had the vasectomy which seemed a big thing then, and remember learning through the acrid smell of burning flesh, the importance of diluting TCP before putting it on to the man bits.

But I'd had nothing like this.
There was a background hum of Air Conditioning, the gentle hissing of the Old man's gas, and his occasional whimpering, along with occasional giggling from the ward staff which made me think that for me, this is huge, and yet for them, this whole thing is all so normal….and I should be reassured, after all, by this time tomorrow, my Cancer will have gone.

I got off to sleep around three, and slept soundly until six thirty.

<u>Day twenty one – OPERATION DAY It's finally arrived!</u>

Yesterday was a long miserable day. Today it's get on with it so I've adopted an " up and at 'em " approach to the day. Get on with it. Be practical. It's too late to worry about anything, and now it's up to them. The real experts I mean, those skillful surgeons, anesthetists, and nursing staff, who are about to save my life.

I started the proceedings off with the usual early morning toilet visit, so very important to me, and the last unaided dump I would be having for some time, and a big part of my mental preparation. I realize that something as trivial as this would probably be like shelling peas to trained nursing staff, but it was still very important to me. I showered, clean my teeth, and had the last wet shave I would have for some time, again due to the risk of possible infection.

This was me doing my best to be as prepared as possible.

A nurse came round for a final check. Was I wearing nail varnish, or a wig? Had I nominated a next of kin? Apparently I'm first in theatre, but from all these questions, I was wondering what kind of theatre it was. Was I in panto?
 I'd been told it's a seven hour operation, and the Surgeon will arrive at around eight thirty to do a final briefing. All the time I'm trying to think, that, finally, this is it, and it's really that simple,
I'll have the anesthetic, I'll then wake up and the Cancer will be gone.
It's my focus, *it's why I'm here*, and gives me the opportunity to watch my kids get older and become more perfect than they already are.

More to the point, it allows me to look after Helen in her old age. Very important, I'd seen her driving….

Happy Larry was right about one other thing, (another gem of wisdom dropped in just before lights out the night before, and just before I nipped over to his bed to suffocate the bastard with a pillow! *Well the thought was there.*)

There are no guarantees in life. I might walk out of here, hobble out of here, or go out in a wheelchair, and another type of Cancer might be waiting round the corner. If it is, I simply start fighting.
But I might just as easily walk in front of a bus, (or hobble or lose control of the above wheelchair), or be at the airport when the really smart suicide bomber turns up.

Who knows? It's often about luck, and I remember those poor folks up in Lockerbie watching the television when an airplane landed on their house.

At this moment in time, this is the only way to go for me.

A nice Asian doctor arrived, the anesthetist, and explained his part in the procedure, emphasizing that I would have an epidural for at least the first twenty four hours, which helped enormously given the worry I had about pain. I thought that I wish I hadn't done the suicide bomber jokes, which seem a bit tasteless right now. Helen arrived promptly at eight, and helped me get ready, firstly the gown which I was told fastened at the back, and then some little white knickers.

"They'll be for ripping off when the operation starts." she points out.

"I'd feel a lot better if it was you who were wearing them....!" I want to respond.

And then we were off, wheeled down to Theatre, on the bed, alongside a new anesthetist, Saffi. Her opening gambit, accompanied by a glint in the eye, was,
"Don't mess with me, I'm bossy!" She immediately put me at ease.

"Now, have we got a wedge for the patient?" I was secretly hoping the knock out stuff would have been administered by a syringe, but medical science moves on and obviously, a crack over the head from a low handicap golfer does the trick.... So,

I replied," No, but I've a sand wedge in the back of the car, and Helen's taking me home, so I suppose that would make her the driver...."

I suppose panic was setting in, and the whole thing was getting to me. But what was obvious was that this lot had done this before.

"Put your hands on your chest please ", I was told by the guy pushing the trolley. "We don't want yet another accident...*we don't do bogof* operations at this hospital mate!" (Yet another comedian, buy one, get one free, I'm in a supermarket...madness.)

I was then introduced to a third anesthetist, a tall sallow youth called Lee. I remember asking," You've done this before haven't you?" to which he replied,
"Yes, I've learned a lot since I started here last week as an apprentice."

(Trust my luck, a GNVQ anesthetist. It was so well rehearsed, and comforting, and very surreal at the same time...)

"We'll put you to sleep now", he says, all serious for a moment.... "I have tried telling stories to patients, 'cos people tend to fall asleep when I tell stories. I'm sure a boring storyteller....", he twinkled.

He places the oxygen mask over my face and the last words I remember hearing are" Take deep breathes while I count to ten, One, two, ..." ,

....and I was gone!

<u>Time out.</u>

I'd made it so far, and I like to think that during this time, I'd managed to stay as cheerful as I could possibly be. Unfortunately, seven hours later, after I'd regained consciousness, what followed can only be described as some of the most miserable weeks of my life.

It was a roller coaster ride, one minute up, the next minute down, and the things that we'd been warned about that could go wrong, did go wrong…all of them.

There were complications all the way through conspiring to make this, my most miserable summer ever.

I have to say now, that I would certainly recommend writing a book to anyone in a similar position. It focuses the mind, and I have thoroughly enjoyed the last two and a half weeks, talking to new and old acquaintances, revisiting memories long forgotten, but I'd like to continue with my recovery story because first of all, it's good for me, because I feel better just by putting the words on to paper, but mainly, because I owe it to the people who have supported me through the next part of the journey, family, friends, and the top surgical specialists and amazing nurses, who do this daily at the Royal Orthopedic Hospital, Birmingham.

But let's be honest, I'm getting through this because deep down, *I really am a tough bugger*, and beating Cancer is very much about not giving up.
Where I've been really blessed, by somebody's God I suppose, is that to help me get through this, I have been given real support, the care of family and friends, and the skills and expertise of the real experts. But there's still a way to go.

<u>Day one :- The road to recovery.</u>

I woke up to find my world had changed once more.

My name is now William. Not Billy or any Venezuelan equivalent, but quite formally and officially William McCourt.

I did try to tell every doctor and nurse I met, that I am usually called Billy, *but gave up after about three days*.

It was a waste of time.

It no longer mattered to anyone but me.

In my new world of "the hospital", the ward staff, there was constant change. the nurses changed over frequently, the doctors changed over frequently, there were the different shift patterns, and simply, in those first few days, it was evident that no-one had the time to get to know the "Billy".

I was now in "The System".

As Happy Larry had said, "You're one of us now!", and I hate to say it, but he was right.

There I was, in a hospital gown, with a bracelet on my left wrist that said "William McCourt, date of birth 1955" and a notice above my bed labeled "William McCourt". My medical records were all "William McCourt", and so was the name on the notice board in the nurses office pointing out to all and sundry which bed I was in.

I had stopped being me, Billy McCourt the person, and had become the new me, William McCourt the patient.

I was a lump of meat that needed mending, in much the same way that a mechanic fixes a car that's broken. To him, a car is only so much metal, whereas the owner of the car might look longingly at his or her pride and joy, and be daft enough to give it a name, even a personality, occasionally, the sad ones among us may or may not decorate it with pink plastic leather upholstery, stick on the latest in fashionable spoilers, and put in an extremely loud and annoying music system.

And why do girls always give their first cars a stupid name?

Who in their right mind would call a fifteen year old Ford Fiesta, Gladys?

I digress once more. I was simply a slab of meat that needed to be fixed and to these people, I was nothing more than a job of work. The unnecessary complications of having to get to know the "me", the Billy McCourt the person, wasn't important because to them, I'd be in, taken care, and out, never to be seen again….or is that too cynical?

Was it really that simple? Because if it is, it's a sad world we live in.

I'd like to think that what really goes on is this.

Hospital people, in their everyday world, see all manner of death and destruction, broken bodies of the worst possible kind, and to emotionally function, maybe the safest course, purely to maintain their sanity, is to maintain distance, and not to get involved.

Whatever the reasons, it really doesn't matter.

I had become William McCourt, the patient, and it didn't feel comfortable. I'm more than that.

Here's what happened next.

My first thoughts on coming out of the anesthetic in the recovery room, were, as you can image, a trifle confused. Not surprising as I'd been out for about seven hours. I was as high as a kite on the concoction of drugs I'd been given, and not at all of the real world, All I initially remember was feeling very cold, and shivering from top to bottom, and remember having a really terrible thirst.

Yet, despite this, my first instinct was to look down and count up to two…feet I mean. I had this overwhelming urge to make sure that nothing had gone wrong during the operation, and that both legs were present and correct. I could feel both feet, but had heard somewhere in the dark and distant past that you could have phantom pains and feelings after an amputation.

So I checked, and an overwhelming feeling of relief washed all over me!

Around this time, I also had a vague recollection of someone giving me the instruction, "Now wiggle your toes!", which apparently I did, and successfully at that. This sort of gave me the warm reassurance that all had gone well.

I don't remember much else. I think I slept.

Sometime, later that first day, I was moved out of the recovery room to the High Dependency Unit, where it's usual to stay for one, or possible two nights to monitor the first stages of recovery and get you over the worst, where apparently I started slipping in and out of sleep, and dozed on and off for a fairly long passages of time.
When I next woke up, I was given some oral morphine and told I could have as much as I needed, and thought here was

my chance to see if you really do get a high out of drugs. I was disappointed.

I don't see what all the fuss is about. It's not a patch on jogging.

But the relief to know I was back, and intact, was enormous.

Also, for some inexplicable reason, I felt the need to know everything about every tube and piece of equipment I was attached to. Looking back, I suppose this was my way of trying to reassert some sort of control over a situation I had no control over, or maybe to give me back some individuality given as how all these strangers were calling me William all the time.

Maybe it was simply my first attempt to be positive.

"What's that machine over there doing?", I remember asking someone.

"It pumps things," was the vague reply. They were busy and had obviously met the village idiot before.

"What's this stuff I'm breathing?", I ask yet another nurse.

"It's oxygen and a mixture of some mild opiates…sort of painkillers", she said, *and in a single moment, simply by taking the time to explain to me, simply being talked to like a normal human being, I'd felt I'd won some sort of minor victory, a sort of, "there, it was a reasonable question to ask, wasn't it", and," I'm really not that stupid", and there really is a person here after all.*

Did I mention the drugs?

177

Laura, Claire and Carl had spent the day with Helen visiting Cadbury Chocolate World, and I had been totally adamant that I didn't want any of them to see me like this.

I was their big strong Dad for God's sake, and I didn't much like the idea of them seeing me helpless and hooked up to tubes and machines. Besides, I'd gotten it into my mind that getting through this was something I simply had to do for myself. It's a man thing. It's about pride…

I didn't have much choice in the matter though, when Helen and the kids walked in through the door. Not totally unexpected though. When did they ever take any notice of me growing up?

They put on a brave face, smiled a lot, but I could tell that seeing me like this had upset them. To their credit, they hid it well. Actually, Carl didn't come in at all. He was feeling starry eyed and sweating a lot seeing as how he'd *overdosed on chocolate,* which sort of meant that the two of us were as high as kites.

"Did you bring me any chocolate?", I remember asking.

"Yes, but it's going to be rationed", replied Helen.

You would think that in the position I was in, I could expect at least a small amount of leeway regarding the food intake, a little sympathy and tenderness?

"You've got to lose more weight".

The C word came to mind again…the other nasty vegetable one.

Anyhow, I felt much better after my next little sleep, and was really glad to see Helen when she walked in for the second time, feeling a little less zonked….me that is!

I think it's important to mention at this point, that in the short time I'd been awake, I'd made yet another incredible discovery… *aren't catheters amazing.*

I didn't realize that you don't even feel the urge to have a pee! It sort of just happens without you ever knowing about it. Amazing! I had the thought that if they had them in pubs, maybe linked up to the bar stool, you need never leave the bar again….just plug yourself in, and off you don't go…. I'm blaming the drugs for these strange thoughts!

But things were still quite serious.

The High Dependency Unit, or H.D.U. is a pretty serious place to find oneself, and is there to provide a very high level of care to post operative patients like myself. One nurse is directly responsible for two or sometimes three patients only, and is constantly kept busy looking after their individual needs, and given that I had two tubes in my hand, one in my arm, one in my neck, one in my back, a monitor on my finger, a drain from my wound, and the catheter, there was a lot to monitor.

I found it a bit of a scary place at first.

Helen had settled herself in the chair next to me and I remember feeling reassured at the sound of rain on the window outside. It reminded of me of our caravan, and how snug we'd feel, with the soft lights, and the glow of the fire when the rain pounded the roof.

"I've had Chilli for tea. I'd better not kiss you! ",I vaguely remember Helen saying, and thinking it was a bit of a daft

179

thing to come out with considering the state I was in, but everything about today was a bit surreal. She'd also started wiping every surface she could see with antiseptic wipes to keep infections at bay, her way of staying in control, and she stayed with me while I drifted in and out of sleep.

Sometime during the day, she'd gone over to the main ward to pick up some stuff for me, and unluckily, had bumped into Happy Larry.

"I see what you mean about him," she points out, "he's spooky".

Not a "How's he doing?", or "I hope the operation went ok". Oh no, not him.

"He's one of us now! ", he'd pointed out to Helen, in what he'd probably thought was his best reassuring manner. I remember thinking that I hope his bloody leg falls off....bastard.

Just before dozing off once more, I was given a blood transfusion because things weren't quite sorted out properly yet, and remember touching what I thought was a huge plaster cast over my stomach, feeling nothing at all, due to the fact that I was still being given an I.V. epidural.

It didn't seem anything to be overly concerned about.

Much later, Helen said her goodbyes and wondered over to her pad in the nurses quarters to spend her second night without a cuddle, and I tried to go to sleep, but couldn't. I tried to settle myself down for the night, but it was all so alien. The guy in the bed next to me sounded like Darth Vader with his oxygen mask on, and all around me, little alarms were going off when the other patient's I.V. bags needed changing. I wasn't in any

180

great pain because of all the drugs that I was banging into myself, so deep down felt quite optimistic, despite it being very early days.

It was more the fact that I was having to sleep on my back for the first time in my life and I just couldn't. I didn't realize that it would be months before I'd have a really good night's sleep.

But I'd survived the first day.

<u>Day Two.</u>

After what I can only describe as a good first day, probably due to the high level of drugs I'd been given, a little bit of reality was starting to kick in.

I was still very ill, and now had a substantial amount of pain to deal with. I was learning how to control the amount of epidural in that two bleeps from the alarm meant I'd given myself was usually enough to sort it out. On top of this I could still have any amount of oral morphine and I took this at the first sign of discomfort to keep even the slightest amount of pain at bay.

I wasn't taking any chances.

Still, I found it difficult to get comfortable and could feel every little crease in the bed.

I was a mess. All of my right hand side, from pelvis to toes had swelled up to double their normal size The man veggies had swollen to the size of small turnips, not a wrinkle in sight, as a result of the operation and were really, really, very really, uncomfortable. Not surprising seeing as how they'd literally chopped my leg off, and then put in back on again. The scar that had been left behind was nothing like Bob's tidy little number. This one started in my groin and went all the way round to the inside of my sexy little bum. Another two inches and they might as well have used a chain saw. It was amazing really.

"Helen, can you please, please, please, give my man bits a scratch, they're driving me mad, "I pleaded.

"I'm not going anywhere near them! ", she answered, with a look of horror on her face. "You can't see the size of them from where you're at!"

Our big regret to this day is not taking a photograph of them for the family album.

They were something again!

(Actually, she waited until the nurses weren't looking, and did give them a bit of a scratch. It must be true love!)

But the process of beating this thing was starting with the small challenges, the insignificant little things that wouldn't have even crossed my mind a week ago.

I mean, my first target was to make myself more comfortable by pulling myself up the bed, and successfully managing it for the first time, using the bed head and monkey bars, was a major achievement.

But I did it, and it was a start,

This was the way it would be for many months to come, making tiny, tiny steps at a time, but I didn't realize this right away. What was becoming very apparent was that the little things we so often take for granted, were now either impossible, or had become huge obstacles, often way out of reach to begin with, but would become ever more achievable, again through tiny, tiny steps.

One example is that of just being able to tie my shoelaces. I would take over four months before I could do it.

What was becoming clear was that my life had changed.

Mr Grimer, the Consultant came round early this morning to tell me that everything had gone really well, like clockwork in fact, and as far as they were concerned, the Cancer had been cut out and was gone.

Brilliant news.

Obviously, they will have to wait for the results of the biopsy to be certain, but for the meantime, there was nothing to worry about. He also said that for the foreseeable future, I would be feeling very weak, and therefore rest was the order of the day. When I take my first steps out of bed, in about a weeks' time, I would need to wear a brace, for about six weeks at least, from waist to knee, to limit my range of movement in the short term, which it turn would help prevent any dislocation.

Good news indeed, all very well and good, and very reassuring, *but he'd said nothing about the most important news I was desperate to hear.*

"Mr Grimer, what about my sex life? ", I desperately asked.

He looked at me with a worried expression, a little confused, because I could see him thinking, what on earth my sex life had to do with him, until he realized what I was getting at.

"No problem at all", he beamed, "We managed to stay well away from the nerve that affects the man thing",…or words to that effect!.

"YABBA DABBA DOO!!!", I quietly scream, like I could imagine Fred Flintstone doing if he got similar news, all in my head! So, So, So much, much, more reassuring.

To celebrate, I ate a cheese sandwich.

This was the first food in two days and tasted marvelous, despite the fact it was the healthy wholesome brown bread variety, and contained celery. Other than this, the rest of the day was sort of spent drifting in and out of sleep, and pressing the epidural button as and when I needed it.

Helen's Mum and Dad had decided that a bit of support was needed in the McCourt household, and had traveled down to Birmingham during the day, and set up camp in their campervan at a small site about five miles from the hospital, to be near us should we need them. I was really very touched, and remember thinking that it's only at times like these that we find out really what family is all about.

For weeks now, I'd been worrying about how all this would affect Helen, and so apparently were the rest of the family.

This is what real support in a time of crisis should be, and like I said before, and can't say it enough, I've been blessed with one amazing family.

<u>Day Three.</u>

I've had a bad night. I am still having trouble trying to sleep on my back, and spent the whole night wanting to turn on my side, and couldn't. This has meant that the longest I've managed to shut my eyes and sleep is about an hour at any one stretch.

What also didn't helped was the real feeling of discomfort I was having.

I woke up feeling awful and neglected.

Helen came in at around eight o'clock and I quickly find out I'm not the only one who's had a bad night sleep. She hadn't slept properly for worrying and the stress of the previous forty eight hours had obviously taken its toll. Not a great start to the day.

The first job was getting me cleaned up, and involving my very first bed bath which took the best part of an hour. I'd sort of been looking forward to this…ok not really, but it meant having the nurses washing all the unimportant bits, with me being responsible for the very important bits. I also had to learn to clean my teeth lying down, and spitting into a cardboard bowl and found this difficult without dribbling everywhere.

But afterwards, I felt much better.
What followed next was pure torture, namely, the changing of the sheets.

A necessary task to stop a patient from getting bed sores, it involved being rolled onto my good side, by three nurses, and rolled back again when the sheets had been changed. This was pure agony, and was why the young lad, who I'd spotted on

186

my first visit to Birmingham, had screamed so loudly. The sound of groaning and moaning, as the sheets were changed, was a regular background noise in the ward, and the news that it hurt everyone, and not just me, wasn't comforting in the slightest.

The bad news was that, by now, my stomach felt uncomfortable and distended and although it felt that it was time to have one thing I'd been dreading for weeks, namely the first bowel movement, unfortunately, nothing much seemed to be happening.

I had the totally unrealistic picture in my mind that I could hold it in for a few days until I could get to the toilet on crutches and sort myself out. Very unrealistic and very naïve.

"I'll be glad when they take this plaster cast off my stomach, "I remember saying to Helen.

"What plaster cast? ", Helen replied.

"What do you mean? This one, here on my stomach! ", I point out, wondering to myself why is she acting so peculiar. I mean, there was only one cast, and it was round my stomach. To me, it seemed fairly obvious....

"Billy, you haven't got a plaster cast round your stomach! ", I hear, and immediately know something is wrong. I drop my hand to my waist, look Helen in the eye, and say to Helen, "What's this then? ".

"That IS your stomach! "

"Oh dear!" I said, (Or words to that effect....we've been here before!)

And so began the most miserable week of my life. Not only was I completely constipated and blocked up solidly at one end, but also had what was called a paralytic ileum…meaning that I was blocked at both ends, and my stomach had blown up like a balloon.

I felt like I was having triplets at the very least, and had only been given one day's notice that I was pregnant.

The duty doctor decided that enemas and laxatives were needed, (whereas I was more in favour of Semtex and other forms of plastic explosive), and an X-ray was suggested to see if surgery was needed to sort the problem out.

I was in agony and the day just dragged on.

After I'd had the X-ray, it was decided I would need to be aspirated, which means having a tube put through the nose and down into the stomach, and believe me, this is not as easy as it seems. On the first attempt, I vomited everywhere. I did the same on the second attempt, and early into the evening, I finally managed to get a smaller diameter tube down into my stomach. (I thought of John Newnes at College and his party trick, and thought that if I was him, I wouldn't be having anything like this amount of trouble). A very large syringe was then attached onto the end of the tube, and the bile was syringed out every two or three hours or so.

No more food. Instead, I was now attached to I.V. solutions, and allowed an ice cube to suck every so often.

I clock watched, and the seconds dragged by. All I could think was that I would get through this ordeal. The lower blockage was painful, and I learned quickly that constipation, the butt of many jokes, was seriously no laughing matter.

At one point I was so miserable, I whispered in my lovely wife ear,

"Helen, if you really love me, you would get a rubber glove from one of the nurses and stick your finger up…..".

I was desperate….and it didn't happen.

But, at 12.30 a.m., I did a tiny little bowel movement. I texted a message to Helen, "Hooray, hooray, the eagle has landed".

Helen texted a message to the kids," Yippee, yippee, dad's had a Poo!"

But alas, it was a false dawn. Everything closed down, and time dragging took on a whole new meaning.

Days Four, Five and Six...I think!

Sometime on the fourth day, the aspirating tube blocked up, and I vomited the whole thing out, *and the shock of it wrapping round my tonsils on the way out scared the living daylights out of me.*

I was frightened of it happening again, and, try as hard as I might, I couldn't get the tube back down into my stomach again, no matter how hard I tried. Every nurse who tried had a different technique which they swore by, but alas, I wasn't having any of it.

This meant that every four hours, the bile in my stomach would back up, and I would spew the whole lot out again, and would continue to do, day and night, so for the next two days. Pure green bile, like in the film, "The Exorcist", but, in my mind's eye, it was infinitely better than having the tube put back down.

Unfortunately, every time I spewed, the sheets would need to be changed, causing more pain and misery each time I was rolled over.

My aim however, when throwing up, got significantly better, and I could hit the tray I was given to puke into, fairly accurately as time went on. This sounds silly, but was important, because it meant that I didn't have to have the sheets changed, didn't have to be rolled, and didn't have to suffer the pain that went along with it.
I was having enemas, and taking laxatives which promptly came straight back up again, and had no effect.

Nothing would shift the blockage, and the clock continued ticking.

More worrying still was that there was blood in my urine, and the Consultant had come round to inform me that there were signs of infection in the wound, the very thing we'd been warned about that we didn't want to happen. There was now the very real possibility that I may lose the leg.

I felt helpless.

Sometime during day five, we managed to get the tube back down. It was sheer murder, and the nursing staff began to worry about the bile reaching my lungs, given the continuous vomiting.

If that happened, apparently I'd be in real trouble.

The three to four hour removal of bile by syringe started up again, bringing a little relief.

I was in hell. Shifts changed, people passed by, alarms rang, and it all became one long blur.
Laura came to visit on day six, and apparently, so did Auntie Patricia, but I have little recollection of either of them being there.

On various days of that week, Helen's parents had brought their campervan to the hospital car park, and were there for her to go and have a little respite from my torment, and have a welcome cup of tea, (Or maybe it was vodka, God knows, she deserved it?)

I was also developing an obsession with fruit and fruit juice, and all I could think of was how wonderful the first smoothie would taste when I was through this. Never again would I allow the taste of a bacon sandwich to pass by my lips.....my body is a temple.

I was in Hell!

And yet there were times when I smiled.

I was beginning to get to know the different styles of caring that my nurses had to one another. Margaret kept me going with very kind words, and ice cubes, and the professionally assertive manner which all the nursing staff had, supported and cajoled me through this miserable time in what could only be described as pure professionalism.

Sharon was blond. Well actually, she was a West Indian lady, but her totally laid back and giggly manner, and the way she often left things behind on the bed when she'd finished doing her thing was pure blond.

She made me laugh.

But I will never forget George.

In the next bed, an eighty seven year old man who'd just had a hip replacement, was also struggling.

His name was George, and he was visited regularly by his two sons who couldn't ever be mistaken for anyone else when you saw them all together, because of their identical monk haircuts. I was having a difficult enough time of it, but at least I knew who I was, where I was, and that I was alive.

There were times when poor old George didn't.

"Can you spit out George? ", I heard a nurse ask, and out flew his false teeth to the other side of the Ward.

This was followed not long after by George pointing crying out, "I've died, oh dear, I've died ", after coming round from a nap. He'd obviously had a very bad dream, and it took the nurses ages to convince him that he was in fact still alive. He seemed very disappointed.

And, shortly afterwards, George made his bid for freedom, where, after ripping out all his tubes, he tried to make it out of his chair and off into the sunset, an amazing feat for a man of his age, and given the state he was in. His voice was filled with pure anguish when he realized he couldn't make it.

He didn't really know where he was, and it was quite sad really, but the real reason I will never forget George was overhearing a conversation he was having with his wife in the early hours of the morning.

Not that unusual except for the fact that *she had died a few years previously.*

(Ok, I appreciate that I was under substantial stress during this time, and was still on a varied diet of drugs, but I swear, that at two in the morning, George was actually talking to his wife.)

And what was even weirder was that it wasn't the voice of an old man!

It was what can only be described as the youthful and happy voice of a very young man, perhaps someone in their early twenties, having a warm and loving conversation with a lighthearted female. Yes, there were two very distinct and different voices, deeply locked in what I can only describe as the memory of loving conversation from many years before.

It was bizarre. It was very moving, and I felt I was eavesdropping where I shouldn't have been.

It really did happen.

193

As to where I was, although there were no signs of the Earth moving, I was slowly improving. My urine was now the color of a good malt whisky, and no longer the color of Guinness, which both Helen and I took to being a good sign. I much prefer a small malt whisky to a pint of Guinness.

Chris, my somersaulting, tree hugging, cycling mate also came to visit today, and it was nice to see him. He very kindly brought me some books to read, and a get well card. Now, for the record, and he may deny this, but I still think that the main reason he came to visit me was to get away from his in-laws, where he was staying for a couple of nights, not far from the hospital.

Apparently they both have Alzheimer's, and wake up each morning, glaring at each other, not knowing who the other one is, They then accuse each other of breaking and entering, and threaten each other with the police, in what I can only imagine as a daily nightmare.
Once again, due to the drugs and discomfort, I remember little about his visit. I do remember it was nice to see him though.

Claire also came down about this time for a visit, with Carl in tow because Claire had missed the train, and he'd kindly offered to drive her to the next railway station.
Unfortunately, he finished up driving the whole two hundred miles to Birmingham.

In their usual thoughtful way, they also brought presents to cheer me up.

They brought crayons and children's coloring books in case I got bored.

Again, unfortunately, I can recall little of these visits.

My final visit of the day was from Richard the Physiotherapist, who was given the task of starting me out on the road to recovery. He tried very hard to put me in the picture about what would be happening in the immediate future, introduce me to a few basic exercises, and give me a bit of a pep talk.

It was all a waste of time really. He then had to repeat it all the following week.

And sometime during these couple of days, because the whole week was really something of a haze, I spotted Dr Bakhir, my consultant from back home in Scarborough, walking through the ward.

"What are you doing here?" I asked, surprised to see him here.

"I work down here!" he replied, looking at me as if I'd lost my marbles.

"It's nice to see you again. I never thought I'd see you down here in Birmingham", I say, and it was nice to see him, because it was Dr Bakhir who had spotted something wrong with the initial X-ray, and it was he who had first mentioned Cancer over the phone when my first lot of results had come back. He set the whole Birmingham thing in motion, so quickly, and can take a lot of the credit in catching this thing so early.

He continued to look at me strangely.

"You do remember I was your anesthetist during your operation?" he asked.

I hadn't had the slightest idea.

He had visited me on the morning of the operation and probably because he was wearing his surgical gown and hat, and not the shirt and tie he wore on my hospital visits in Scarborough, I'd simply not recognized him.

That, and the fact I was probably a hell of a lot more stressed than I realized. I've a lot to thank him for… *and didn't realize that I'd be thanking him a lot more in the not too distant future.*

This was also the day that Helen and I had our first argument in weeks.

Silly really.

I'd been given a lovely basket of fruit from friends and former teaching colleagues at Pinder School, Scarborough, but was still on nil by mouth. It had been delivered to Ward 12, the Cancer ward, where, had all gone well where I should now be recovering, and I was suddenly overwhelmed with the desire to make sure all that lovely fruit wouldn't go to waste, and wanted Helen to give it to the other patients on the ward, seeing as how I wouldn't be on solid food for the foreseeable future.

She wanted to wait until I got out of the H.D.U. and could have some of it myself, but, oh no! I was having none of it.

The whole episode completely blew up out of proportion, and the whole thing turned into one massive issue in my mind. In my defense, I think it was, once again, my way, of trying to reassert some kind of control, and an attempt at not feeling so totally helpless. She left the ward upset, and once I'd calmed down, I quickly saw how stupid I was being.

I just wasn't thinking straight.

The week had almost passed, and had been a blur. All sense of time, despite the fact it was still passing minute by minute, second by second, had been lost.

I was living from aspiration to aspiration, ice cube to ice cube, and being turned regularly.

I had no idea what was happening in the outside world, and cared even less. I'd sort of gotten lost in my own particular form of misery and was finding it hard to find my way out.

<u>Day Seven.</u>

What can I say? Just this…

I pooed three times during the night, and the sense of relief was overwhelming… another Fred moment…"Yabba dabba doo".

I was delighted, Helen was delighted, and the kids were delighted. Andrew later said he received a text message notifying him that dad had just had a Poo, and him, and his mates, thought it hilarious, and fell about laughing, seeing he was having a drink in a bar in Greece at the time.

And, what was more, for the next few days, *I was praised every time I'd fart.* (It's strange how the novelty seems to have worn off by now, all I get these days is a wrinkled up nose and a withering look.)

But at last, it looked like the episode was over and it was all downhill from here….*or so I thought!*

Helen's Mum and Dad made their first visit to the ward, despite the fact that they'd been here the whole week. It was lovely to see them, just to say thanks. They had been tremendous.

And suddenly, things were starting to look up.

As the day progressed, most of the tubes were removed from various parts of my body, the last one being the aspirator. (I actually removed it myself, offering some lame excuse that I'd coughed it up. I'd just had enough), and later in the day, it was "Goodbye H.D.U.".

I'd thanked everybody as best I could, but it just didn't seem enough, given the amount of support and care I'd been given, and despite the various tins of chocolate biscuits that Helen had handed over during the week.

I suppose this was just the normal way that things get done in a hospital.

I was then transferred back to Ward 12, the Cancer ward, and just being outside in the fresh air albeit for a few brief moments, had a sort of "holiday feel" to it.

A thought entered my head though. If there had been no Cancer, I'd be now in Italy for the long summer holidays, but somehow, for some inexplicable reason that I couldn't quite put my finger on, it just didn't matter!

I was just so glad to be out of the H.D.U. I was back to the bed space I'd left a week ago, and the other really bit of good news was that *there was no sign of Happy Larry*. Happy days.

The cancer ward was very different to the H.D.U., in that it had a more relaxed, less frenetic feel to it, very different from the atmosphere of intensive activity of the week before. I'd received a bunch of flowers from my mother which was all a bit weird seeing that this would make me the first bloke in the family ever to receive a bunch of flowers from anyone. Unfortunately, they had to be taken out of the ward straight away, because they smelled of cat's pee. They were lilies, and I suppose they did look lovely if you're into that sort of thing.

She was making a big effort which I appreciated, and besides, Helen appreciated them in her little student room, despite the nasty smell.

I was then given what seemed a mountain of get well cards to open and read, which do cheer you up.

I then spoke to our Andrew for the first time to make sure he was ok, and started setting up my other life support system, the DVD player, the T.V. buttons, and the mobile phone. I had sort of accepted that I'd be spending a lot of time in bed in the foreseeable future, and boredom would be something I'd have to watch out for.

I then spent hours answering the hundred and twenty seven text messages I'd received over the past week.

Now that systems were back and working again, I was now allowed a soft food diet which I would have to follow for the next twenty four hours, consisting of soup, more soup, and ice cream, and it all tasted great. Helen had brought in some fruit smoothies which I attacked with mucho gusto, and these were simply the nicest thing I've ever tasted.

Not surprising seeing it had been over a week since I last eaten.

I'd started noticing a few more things. The two other chaps in the next beds had both had lower leg amputations, and were struggling a little, each in their own way. Despite what I can only describe as the optimistic euphoria I was feeling, I was soon realizing how lucky I'd been in the "contracting Cancer world", compared to some of the other patients on the ward.

The guy two beds down was Maurice, a Yorkshire farmer, who was todaydead chuffed because over the past day of so, he'd made such good progess to the point where he was now walking on crutches and could make it to the toilet unaided, and this just over a week since his operation to remove his leg just below the knee.

I didn't realize at the time how big a milestone this all too familiar activity of going to the loo becomes when, all of a sudden we can't do it. It's horrible.

The other chap, James, was having a much more difficult time of it, finding it very difficult to get comfortable, and most of the time he was in a lot of pain.

I began to see why it was important to get a patient back onto the ward as soon as possible after an operation.

It was reassuring to learn that there was a kind of camaraderie, a sort of spirit of togetherness amongst the patients on the ward, and generally, people wanted to help each other get through what were some difficult times. Progress was easier when there were others in the same boat to help keep spirits up when they began to flag.

On the whole, this had been the best day so far, and found I slept a little better seeing as how I was away from the constant alarms going off all through the night, and also because on this ward, the lights were turned out at night to help patients sleep better.

All in all, I was fairly happy, because, at last, it seemed I was finally making progress, despite being trapped in a hospital bed, away from the outside world, and not being able to function as before. Realistically, I'm still alive and kicking, (ok, maybe not kicking, no, definitely not kicking), but I'm still here on planet Earth, and the fact is that it could have been so much worse.

The insignificant worries of the dreaded bowel movements were long gone. I had faced my worst nightmare, and it wasn't all that bad.

I was now William McCourt, patient, and therefore it was alright to be dependent on others, at least that's what I kept telling myself. These people are professionals, they did their work in a manner that provided a level of dignity to me, the patient, and quite simply, they had seen it all before.

Time out.
I have found writing about this week in the H.D.U. very difficult. To try and remember the sequence of events, I got Helen to write down lots of little notes to remind me of all the things that had happened, but didn't realize it would be a full four months before I would be able to sit at a keyboard with any level of comfort, and try to type up these recollections. I suppose the mind tries to forget times of pain and anguish, and I found that when I started reading Helen's notes, I just couldn't remember some of the events about which she had written.
I guess the mind also heals over time. I suppose it's the body's way of helping us to keep functioning as human beings.

When I recently visited the Hospital for some intensive Physiotherapy, I found that I couldn't face visiting the H.D.U. I'm also guessing that sub-consciously, I'm somehow, at some level, still trying to put the whole of that first week out of my mind..

<u>Day Eight.</u>

Today, I ate my first breakfast.

It just gets better and better.

What really cheered me up though, was that I had my hair washed today for the first time since coming here, not a great deal to shout about you may say, but remember, I'd been vomiting every three or four hours, for days on end, and my hair hadn't been washed at all during that time…. it was a disgusting sight.

Sue, one of the ward nurses, had been a hairdresser at some time in a previous life, and the whole experience of laying back, and having my hair shampooed was just wonderful.

Then came the bed bath, and I felt like a new man, though not in any cowboys in a tent sense,

I felt like I was a new man.

The other bit of really good news came from the other Consultant, who told me that the pathology report had come in, and the results of the tests to see if the Cancer had spread to anywhere else in my body, had come back clear.
The Cancer was gone.

A bit of an anti-climax really given the whole spectrum of emotions I'd gone through for the past few weeks. No trumpet fanfare or fireworks, the tests have come back clear and that was it. Ok, I will still need checking every three months like anyone else who has been diagnosed with cancer, but I'd sort of got used to the idea of cut, chop, gone.

But it was good news, and this, followed by my first cup of tea meant things were definitely looking up.

So, what had been happening in the world…

I'd heard of lot of pitter patter of raindrops during the week I'd been in the H.D.U. and putting the T.V. on for the first time gave me a bit of a shock. I hadn't realize there had been so much rain, although I was aware that Eddie and Marilyn, Helen's mum and dad, had delayed their return to Yorkshire because of the awful weather.

When I saw the floods in Tewkesbury, I felt a little guilty, because the month before I'd just bought a boat was from a bloke in, yes, you've guessed it, Tewkesbury. I got to thinking he probably wished he'd kept hold of it, poor bugger.

And today, I had a visit from Jasper Carrott.

A bit weird really…. Today, the Cancer had finally gone, and here is Jasper Carrott.

I'd always been a bit of a fan, especially of "The Detectives", and his standup routines of the Seventies. The only blot on his copybook as far as I was concerned, was that totally naff "Funky Moped" song, but here he was in person, a real comedy icon, standing at the foot of my bed.

Actually, he was here to officially open the Cancer Ward after a major refurbishment, and to carry out the ceremonial thing, but it was nice the way he took the time to chat to all the patients and the whole thing did cheer me up. The one thing that I thought was also a bit bizarre was the carrot cake the nurses had made him for his lunch, I bet he never saw that one coming, a bit like the Queen always smelling fresh paint wherever she goes, and his visit sort of explained the high number of strange people wandering round the ward carrying empty boxes, or pushing empty wheelchairs, all morning before he arrived.

He's a popular bloke in Birmingham.

He said something about appearing on his T.V. show, something called "Goldenballs", but I'd actually never heard of it. I took the time to watch it on the T.V. the following day.

I thought it was utter tripe.

All I could make out was that the contestants had to lie and con each other about their balls, to get into the final, where the two finalists would cheat and lie to each other so that they both walked away with nothing. I didn't get it!

After "The Detectives", it was just a little disappointing.....

The other funny thing was that whoever had organised buying the plaque on the wall for the occasion had spelt the word "Carrot" with one t., same as the cake, and not "Carrott".

But is it really his real name? I've no idea...

Seeing as today I'm feeling so much better, I feel that it's time to get back on track, and continue the life story bit. Here's another adventure...

At the tender age of forty, I found my "new" brothers and sisters, my other family, who and are all Venezuelan.

Maibe and Myrian live in the United States, and Irma now lives in Spain, and about once a month or so, I spend hours on the phone to Myrian, talking about the family and catching up.

In many ways, discovering them went a long way to making the jigsaw that is my life complete.

You see, three weeks after my Nan died, I suffered a heart attack, at the tender age of forty, me that is, not my Nan. Not pleasant, but no real drama. With Heart Attacks, providing you do the important bit, survive, it's usually done and dusted within days, and we rest up for a while and move on.

The down side therefore was the three month period of recovery where I had to stay at home and take things easy for a while.

I got very, very bored.

For the first six weeks, I had to spend a lot of the time laying down, not exerting myself and the boredom was driving me mad. It seemed a good idea then, to try and find out what had happened to good old biological dad, and if I'm honest, it was something I had always had on the back of my mind to do.

I suppose I hadn't made the effort earlier because I didn't want to upset my Nan, but the timing seemed about right to do it now.

What followed was quite remarkable.

I first of all phoned up the Venezuelan Embassy who put me in touch with their Military Attache.

I explained who I was, and that my father had been in Barrow-in Furness between 1952 and 1955, commissioning a new ship that the Venezuelan Navy were having built,

I was a little taken aback, however, when he mentioned, *that he knew him*!

It was really that simple.

My father was still in the Venezuelan Navy, although now retired, and it followed that after he'd had his illnesses in the Sixties, he'd been moved sideways and given a desk job sorting out what I can only describe as posh Navy hotels for the Navel Officers to rest and recuperate in.
These were located in some of the most beautiful parts of Venezuela, and it seems that everyone in the Venezuelan Navy knew him.

He had also continued to lecture part time, as part of his naval duties, until well into his seventies, and let's be honest, *the Venezuelan Navy is not the biggest Navy in the world.*
What followed was really quite moving.
Apparently he and the rest of the family had spent years trying to find me, but they were looking for Guillermo, the Spanish name for William, and for some reason which I can't fathom to this day, they thought my surname was now Smith. He'd even come over to England on one occasion to do so, but had been told by my Nan, that because my mother had married again, I was living somewhere other than Whitehaven and had a different name.

I remember the time when I'd be about ten years old, being told that there wouldn't be any more contact from Venezuela, and it was time to move, or words to that effect, but hadn't fully grasped the implications.

I often wondered why he had lost contact with me.

The really big surprise was finding out about the siblings.
They had kept a photo album, *of me*, from pictures my mother used to send to him from when I was little, and because of the passionate way that South Americans are where family is concerned, when my brothers and sisters knew I'd been sort of

found, they told me they cried all night. They're big on this sort of thing over there.

Later that year, I went over meet them all, and the first big shock was how short they all were.

We stood back to back in the airport in Caracas looking for one another before we realized who was who. I then found out that I was the image of Uncle Carlos, and it was now obvious where the nose had come from. When I met Uncle Carlos, it was like meeting me, but an older me, twenty or thirty years on, and he was a bald as a coot.
He was a good looking, well preserved sort of bloke, and definitely had something about him.
This gave me a strange, weird sort of satisfaction. I got to thinking that if I looked like him in later life, well then, it wouldn't be at all bad would it?

What was really strange was how quickly it all became so normal, and how very quickly I felt part of the family, even though we were struggling to communicate because of the language differences. I was given a photo of Abby when he was about my age, where he was standing on the deck of a large sailing ship at the South Pole, wearing the identical hat I used to go fell walking in. When I later showed it to my mate Dave, he asked why did I have a photo taken in black and white?

It was me to a tee, taken two years before I was born.

 When I later met Myrian, in Houston, Texas, I swear, after about four days together, we could read each other's minds. It was like we'd known each other forever and the similarities continued.

On the family tree thing, I've also asked Myrian's daughter, my niece, Jesica to find out a little more about where Abby came from because, for sure, it's a very different story to the Whitehaven one.

It could be interesting.

Later that evening, I spotted the new arrivals to the ward, in for their final assessments, the way I'd arrived on ward 12 what seemed years ago. The nervous look was there in the eyes of each prospective patient, as was the look of concern in the eyes of their partners, and it was very obvious that they were going through the wide range of emotions I'd been going through weeks earlier. They were busy keeping themselves to themselves, not mixing much with the patients on the ward, not realizing that very soon, they would also become "one of us now", and soon, "enter the system".

There was not a lot to say to them, even if they'd want to listen. Their world would be changing soon enough, as mine had done....

<u>Day Nine.</u>

Sleeping was still causing me problems. No matter how hard I tried, I still couldn't sleep for longer than an hour at a time on my back, so this morning, I was feeling very tired. My body is still very much coming back to normal, one minute very cold and shivering, the next, very hot and clammy. When I do fall asleep, I often wake up in a real sweat.

I'm putting it down to recovery.

What's more, the swelling round the wound is still massive because the rest of my body has sent all the good stuff to my pelvis to help fix it.

I'm also farting like a train, aftershocks from all the laxatives and stuff I'd absorbed over the past week.

It has all the makings of a beautiful day, because this is to be my first day out of bed, and apparently, once I can get up onto my feet, either with a zimmer frame, or crutches, I've been told that the swelling to my thigh, and more especially, my man bits, should start to go down.

They are still huge!

I couldn't do this until the brace arrived. I waited impatiently all morning and early in the afternoon, I was presented with this contraption which consisted of a huge Velcro belt which I put around my waist, a wide band of soft material i put around my thigh, and there was a stainless steel bar in between the two to stop me from bending. This was supposed to prevent the sort of movement which could cause a dislocation.

It felt very restrictive, and I felt very clumsy.

But it didn't matter. It was time to learn to walk again.

Very slowly, I edged to the side of the bed and sat up, with my legs dangling, and got my first surprise of the day.

I was utterly exhausted. Just sitting up had made me feel very dizzy, not what I expected at all.

I did about five steps out from the bed using a zimmer frame, and five steps back again, which was a little scary, my first venture into the unknown, so to speak and on either side of me were two physiotherapists in case I fell.

I felt intimidated and a little emotional.

These were my first steps as a Bionic man, and they were big steps to take.

I found it quite hard going, I felt nauseous, whether through the effort or the fear, I'm not sure, and thought I was going to be sick. But apparently it was normal to feel this way after what I'd gone through, and the two physiotherapists seemed happy with the way it had gone. On the whole, once I'd recovered, I felt quite good too.

A little later, Auntie Patricia came to visit, and it was lovely to see her. She took Helen out for some lunch, and the whole atmosphere for the rest of the day was upbeat and positive. Things were going well.

But then came some bad news, quite ironic as it happened, because the main News story on the BBC this morning had been all about the rise in hospital infections, *and how it's out of control.*

The latest blood test showed that because my stomach had swollen up to such a level last week, and because of the blockage, some nasty little bacteria had made its way into the wound, and the infection was getting worse. (Not a "Fred" moment, but another "Oh bugger" moment…bugger!)

This meant I was to be moved to an isolation room so as not to infect anyone else, where I would be vehemently attacked with antibiotics, administered intravenously, until the infection cleared up.

The only bit of good news was that I had a T.V. and digibox, all to myself, and there would be no Darth Vaders to wake me up through the night….. brilliant!

That first night in my own room, I sat up for hours, not being able to get off to sleep again, and watched the second week of the Tour de France, enjoying every minute of it. All the time, I was trying to be philosophical about the whole thing, because in the bigger scheme of things, it seemed like a very insignificant setback.

Boy was I wrong!

<u>Day Ten</u>

"Morning Robocop!" came the text message from our Claire.

"Johnnie five is alive", I reply.

It was time to have a variation on the bionic man jokes which were starting to do my head in.

The news today was still about the floods, which by now had spread to Oxford, *and some story about Hari Krishnas trying to save a bullock with B.S.E.*

Apparently, people from all over the world were turning up in Wales of all places, to save "Chandra the Sacred Bullock", from being destroyed. What the hell is a sacred bullock and how on earth, or anywhere else for that matter, could anyone tell it was a "Holy" cow? And what would a "Holy" cow be doing in Wales anyhow?

Am I missing the plot or something?

It wasn't too long ago that we'd destroyed six million of the poor beasts because of an insignificant little infection called Foot and Mouth.

I couldn't see what all the fuss was about.
The poor animal in question didn't look very holy either. I'd expected to see a light brown, saggy skinned creature, with great big eyes, that couldn't be anything else but a gift from the Gods.

But it didn't. It looked like a cow, it slobbered like a cow, and on the news it showed a large crowd, sort of standing round and protesting, waiting expectantly for some sort of a miracle to happen.

213

It didn't, which was a bit disappointing really, especially for Chandra.

Sorry I'm rambling again. My mind is on the move again.

Today, I sort feel it's important to have some targets to work toward, it's the "all about being positive thing" again. My feelings are very different to what they were last week, because last week was all about giving up time, whereas now I feel I have to dig deep and think of days to come.

At this moment, my mind keeps drifting back to the fact that it's our school summer holidays, and the big holidays are the real reason that both of Helen and I went into teaching in the first place. It's certainly nothing about liking kids.

It's a well known fact that teachers really don't like kids, and kids really don't like teachers, ask any of them! Really! It's all about the holidays.

But you know what? It doesn't really matter. It's just another holiday. I never thought I'd ever say that!

I feel though, that this is one of those times in your life where you just have to step outside the real world, and accept you've lost some time. It's just a time thing and really won't go on forever, and one day, pretty soon now, it will end. It's a time to take stock, and look forward to the future, and mentally prepare myself to be the best that I can be for when I leave this place.

Today, I've been thinking a bit more about the family tree thing. It did give me some comfort looking back in time to the family history, although why, I'm really not sure. In the days leading up to coming here I'd talked to Colin about the family

214

tree, read great Uncle Cyril's account of living in Newhouses, Whitehaven's own slum area where my ancestors used to live.

I'd been really moved when I'd learned of family members who had died in such terrible circumstances.

We have our own history of poverty, and have survived it for over two hundred years. It's now something that I'm sort of proud of, not that that makes a great deal of sense, does it? It would have been nice though if the first John McCourt (born 1784), had come from Ireland, I've always liked the Irish, and for years now, I've celebrated Paddy's night more than I've ever celebrated St George's day. And Irish immigrants in those days were often met off the boat in Liverpool and enticed to work in the pits by offers of a job and somewhere to live.

I remember a story Keith, a mate of mine once told me, back in the construction days. He told me the story of Michael, (ok, not his real name, but I can't remember his real name, and Paddy would have been far too obvious), who was having money troubles at the time.

Michael, had told his mate, (who shall be called Seamus...), to go into the pub that the lads all drank in, on the next pay day, to tell everybody that he, Michael that is, had died suddenly. This he did and because all the lads who knew him all thought the world of him, they put their hands in their pockets and, as was the custom in times like this, gave generously when the cap was passed round, so as to send the money to his wife back home, in what should have been her time of need.

Keith almost collapsed when he bumped into Michael later that week in the street and once he'd got over shock, told him that If he ever set foot in that particular pub again, the lads would probably kill him.

Michael, ever the philosopher, replied, something along the lines of, "No they won't Keith, They'll be so happy to see that I'm still alive, they'll soon see the funny side of it all, and I'll be soon forgiven".

Apparently, that was exactly as it turned out.

Nowhere else would you ever find such lovable bare faced cheek.

Besides, it's not as if the Irish had the monopoly on poverty, even though it seems to be fashionable to be descended from "The Old Country". They've just been better at marketing it, given the numbers of Irish Bars dotted around the world.

Seriously though, I started the whole family tree thing with a kind of flippancy I suppose I now regret. I had earlier mentioned "Angela's Ashes", the Frank McCourt novel, without having the slightest idea that not too long ago, and on my own doorstep, dramas had unfolded *which had a place in Hollywood*.

Pit disasters on that scale nowadays would be front page news all over the world, and would be remembered for decades. The three McCourt brothers would be like something out of "Saving Private Ryan". It could be a film of real drama.

No, not "Shaving Private Ryan", I believe that is a different film altogether…

Sometime in the future, I'm going to look more into this.

Anyhow, back to today. I'm still in the system, and it's working well. I'm still William McCourt, patient, and the system continues to function.

Today, I had a visit from a dental nurse, to make sure my teeth were in good condition. It seemed a bit strange after all I'd been through, but I suppose it made sense.

Then I had a visit from the Occupational Therapy nurse, which I found incredibly impressive.

She sat down next to the bed, and for the next hour or so, she went through a whole heap of stuff I hadn't even thought about. Stuff like, how I would need to travel up and down, from home to the hospital, in an ambulance, because I wouldn't be able to sit in a car for more than twenty minutes at a time, and all sorts of what and what not to do when I got home.
She explained to me how, between now and going home, other people like herself who were based back in Scarborough, would sort out aids to help me function round the house, like an upright chair, bed and chair raisers, toilet seat extensions, etc etc, even down to shoe horns to sort my feet out.
They would go into the house and measure up for handrails and step extensions and all manner of equipment. The system had really kicked in.

I then had a visit from the Macmillan nurse who talked about things like, how I would need a Disabled persons' parking permit, and how they would help me with necessary paperwork, like applying for disability allowances and the like. The system again.

All of which brought home quickly the fact that, in the short term at least, *I am actually disabled.*

I am disabled and didn't even realize it.

I'd never even thought about being a disabled person.
Disabled people are those folk who get wheeled up and down

the touchline at football matches, and get all the best seats. Disabled people travel about in minivans.

I can't be disabled….can I?

I'd known that I would be a bit slow getting about while I recovered, a bit like waiting for a broken arm to heal, and once the plaster came off, all would be rosy in the garden again.

I'd never actually considered that I could be disabled for the rest of my life.

It was quite sobering.

Who am I kidding? It was depressing!

And here's another thought.

I suppose, where the actual Cancer is concerned, I haven't had to go through the whole Chemotherapy and Radiotherapy thing, I haven't had to lose my hair, lose massive amounts of weight,(which in my case wouldn't be all bad…), and generally be very ill whilst waiting and hoping to be cured.

I'd simply had it cut out.

Cut. Chop. Gone.

It was fairly simple and straightforward, and a very non dramatic way of joining Lance Armstrong's select club, that of namely, becoming a "Cancer survivor."

I suppose the payback is that, once cured, unlike Lance Armstrong, I can't get back on my bike, and be as good, if not better, than I was before. I've got a chunk of metal inside my hip, albeit, a very expensive piece of metal, and a major muscle detour that will prevent that happening.

It's just pluses and minuses.

The plus is, no bald head and suffering, in some cases, in pain for months, if not years at a time.

The big minus is… I'm disabled.

Over the next few weeks, I'm going to have to get my head round the idea that I may not, in reality will most probably not, be able to do a lot of the stuff I've grown to love over the years. I may not be able to walk the Cumbrian fells on sunny winter days with snow laying as far as the eye can see, with the company of my best mates, or take an active part in cycle trips, and kayaking trips, many of which I've done over recent years, in many beautiful locations.

I suppose only time will tell.

So, while all this lot is sinking, I'll take the time and tell you why I am a Badger…

I am in actual fact, Captain Badger.

It goes like this.
A few years ago now, I went on a staff weekend to the Lakes with other teachers and support staff from Tong School, in Bradford, and the prizes for an orienteering race we'd organized were cardboard badger hats. By the end of the day, we were all sitting in a pub drinking copious amount of very good beer, wearing cardboard badger hats. And so it started; the venerable society of, "The Badgers"…

But this story starts a little earlier than this.

Not long after returning to England, I'd gone back into teaching, not because of any desire to "make a difference", or because I had an insatiable love of children. Nope,

I went into teaching because I had three mouths to feed, and teaching was the nearest job to that of being my own boss that I could think of.

I'd decided I'd had enough of the Construction world, and the idea of working outdoors in a cold English winter didn't compare with the outdoor life in South Africa.

I started teaching at a very challenging school in Bradford.

The being teacher speak for what the Irish would lovingly refer to as a shite school in Bradford. It was horrible.

I won't say I enjoyed my first foray into Education, because I didn't. Schools were going through hard times in the Eighties because when the Conservatives got into power, they buggered things up well and truly. Budgets were cut, teachers went on strike, and in many ways, the Education system of this country took a pounding which I believe it is still recovering from today. The schools that suffered the most were the Inner City Schools. Many were hell holes and in my humble opinion, still are and getting worse! I wasn't sure I'd made a good decision, in fact, *the only good thing that happened during this time was the birth of The Boy.*

My son, Andrew John McCourt, was born on the 16th February 1988, at St Luke's Hospital, Bradford. Once again I was over the moon.

He inconsiderately arrived at about 2.30 a.m. and about an hour later, both him and Helen were wrapped up in plastic sheets, put under umbrellas, and *taken outside in a snow storm*, to another ward. It was an old primitive Victorian hospital, and should have been pulled down years ago, and Helen was one of nine births happening at the same time. There just weren't enough nursing staff on duty that night, and I finished up having to wash Helen down myself, and making her that very important first cup of tea.

I remember thinking, *"I had given up South Africa for this?"*.

"Why did you let Helen give birth at St Luke's?" a colleague asked the following day, when I went back into school,

"It's got the highest child mortality rate of any hospital in the Country!", he pointed out, about two days too late.

It certainly wasn't the comforting and caring experience that we'd experienced in South Africa, but both of them were healthy, and it wasn't long before I got them home, and what a smashing little fella he was.

Sorry, I digressed again. I really didn't like teaching at this time, but the positive outcome was that through what I can only describe my "baptism of fire", I picked up a great deal of the skills needed to survive in teaching today, and it got easier.

During this period, I tried to escape from the classroom by selling insurance, which lasted for about three years. Looking back, this was nothing more that a desperate attempt at making more money to help bring up the family, and wasn't my most successful period. The words "Financial Advisor", and "Crook", are very similar in my vocabulary, given the number of shady characters I met at the time, none of whom I have any wish to remember here.

Slowly and surely, I was sucked back once again into teaching, this time, with a big difference.

I'd decided I was coming back into teaching under my terms.

You see, I actually liked teaching kids. I also like outdoor activity stuff, and had a strong desire to give back to lesser fortunate kids, what I'd been given by my old friend Brian Harris, many years before.

If I was going to go back and work in a school, I was also going to organize the outdoor, out of school stuff, because that was the bit where I would get my enjoyment from.

I was going back under my terms.

What I couldn't stand, and still find difficult to this day, is all the petty bureaucracy that schools seem to thrive on. I was a capable bloke, a caring bloke, and I could get through to kids. Ergo, I was a good teacher, and I like to think I still am, even though my style may not tick all the Ofsted boxes every time they come snooping around putting the fear of God into lesser experienced souls.

Schools aren't or shouldn't be about power dressing and exam results. There has to be a soul there. I like to think that's the bit I'm good at.

Me, and my other Badger mates.

Here's the badger bit....

I'd gotten a job at Tong School, another shite (sorry, challenging) establishment in Bradford where the kids used to spit at Ofsted inspectors. It wasn't all bad then....

Here I was blessed in meeting like minded people and over the next seven or so years, alongside my best mates Dave, Sue, Pete, Steph, Duncan, Doren, Chris, Robin, and many other

222

quality people whose names I'll never forget, we managed, between us, over thirty camping trips, dozens of residential visits to outdoor centres, and weekends with the Duke of Edinburgh people, and weeks away with the Army Youth Team, taking hundreds of kids away from their Inner City council house homes, to the Lake District and, on occasions, the Yorkshire Dales.

It's something I'm really quite proud of.

We'd use my old caravan at Wasdale as a base, and to begin with we'd borrow the camping stuff from a Duke of Edinburgh place in Bradford. We'd land late on a Friday night, give the kids the pep talk about working for each other and all the other drivel we'd tell them so they would behave for the weekend, and put the tents up.

Then it was down to Wastwater Lake, where it was ghost stories, and often a visit to the churchyard, in a very small church at the end of the lake, where we could show the kids some human remains. Someone had scattered the ashes of a loved one, which was quite a common given the beauty of the place, but on this occasion, the 50p for the gas had obviously run out because this poor bugger had only been half cooked, and you could still see bits of femor and the like among the ashes. The kids loved this bit.

It's also worth pointing out that my mate Dave has an instruction in his will, nominating me with the job of taking his ashes up to the top of Scafell Pike and scatter him there, should I be the last one between us to shuffle off. I keep telling him that because it rains all the time up there, he's only going to be washed straight back down again, so if he'll be happy with half way up, I'll do it and it'll save me a bit of a walk…

(I hope I'll be able to take him even half way up, because right at this minute, it sounds like a big call….)

223

"Is that Lake District Sir?", pipes up a voice from one of the girls, one weekend.

"Erm, yes, this is the Lake District"...

"No Sir", she repeated, pointing to the lake itself,

"Is that Lake District? I've heard of Lake District and...".

This wasn't as unusual a question as you may think, given that many of these kids had never left Bradford before. They just hadn't traveled much, a bit like me, all those years ago.

"Hey sir, look over there...that dogs' only got three legs!" We'd often hear, as we drove back onto the campsite. The poor animal had had an altercation with some farm machinery at some time in the past.

"That, boys and girls, is the three legged Lake District Sheepdog, specially bred around these parts because the hills are so steep..." and for a long time afterwards, the kids would believe it....

To keep an eye on the kids at night, we used to organize shifts, so that one or two of us could have an evening off now and then and go to the pub. (This was never a problem. We had one camping weekend where we only had eleven kids, but we had thirteen staff....)

Doren, my old mate, who lost her fight with Cancer a few years ago and who was known affectionately as the mad woman, mainly because of the way she'd fly off the handle, only to finish by laughing uncontrollably at the end of her little episode, had started bringing along her son Craig who wanted to be an Outdoor Leader.

After he'd played his tree hugging games with the kids, and they'd settled down for the night, he'd climb up a tree, just above where the kids were supposed to be sleeping, *and stay there for hours.*

When they thought it was all clear, often they'd try and sneak into each other's tents, to be met with, "GET BACK INTO THAT TENT!".

The kids honestly thought that he slept in the tree all night.

In the summer term, it was a constant roller coaster of shopping, cooking, freezing, thawing, into the minibus off for the weekend and back on Sunday night, and this for six weeks at a time without a day off. I'd cheat a bit, and sneak my own kids on board, so that they could see something of Dad over the weekends, and it was brilliant.

It was years before the school would fork out any money to support us, and we supplemented the weekends by doing fundraising stuff like sponsored bike rides across England, and doing the full length of the Leeds to Liverpool canal. We did the national three peaks, but in a more dignified manner, over three days, and eating and drinking like kings every night.

We had evolved to become the "Adventure Badgers."

For the next few years, the Badgers were and, to a great extent, still are, my social world, a group of like minded school workers who supported each other in a very difficult school. We have Badger hats, T-shirts, dolls, basically, if it's got a badger on it, we have it. We went camping together on many weekends, with kids from school. We holidayed and partied together, with Helen and the kids, and formed bonds that have lasted for many years. I love the Badgers and am proud to be a Badger.

I have hundreds of Badger stories, far too many for now, and who knows, one day I might write my book, "The Badgers".

...time out time again...
Something usually happens to put it all into perspective, when the guardian angel steps in...like tonight, for instance. While I've been tinkering at the keyboard, writing this, over my shoulder, I've been trying to watch the BBC's "Sports Personality of the Year", and a disabled athlete, with two false legs has just won a prize. Amazing in itself really.....but for me, it was about his speech. I really liked his acceptance speech which went something like,"it's not about the disability that makes us disabled, it's about the abilities we possess that makes us able".

It's all about timing, and this little gem of wisdom came just at the right time to put things back into perspective. I was getting too old for running marathons anyhow, and I was already too old to play football. It could be so much worse. It's just another challenge.....and I really do like a challenge.

Day Eleven.

"Would you like some cornflakes for breakfast?"

"Ooh, yes please," thinking I'd much prefer bacon, sausages, eggs tomatoes, mushrooms, fried bread…. it didn't take long to get over the," I'll never eat food that's bad for me again" saga.

I think this is a good sign.

The day had started bright enough, and then something really strange happened.

I had a rigor!

On odd occasions, in the days following the operation, I'd experienced moments of uncontrollable shaking, with all my muscles quivering and shivering, and I'd put these down to the body reacting to the invasive procedure, believing it was the body's way of trying to readjust itself. On the odd occasions they'd happened, they would last only for a few seconds and go away again, and I hadn't had one for a few days now. They had seemed to have gone altogether.

But this episode was very different indeed. I'd started to shake uncontrollably, from head to toe, and this went on for *over forty minutes*. I lay there on my own waiting for it to pass, but after about fifteen minutes, I knew I had to ring the alarm. My blood pressure had dropped significantly, and I was put back on oxygen, and for a short while, my temperature was out of control. I was wrapped up in blankets because if felt really very cold, and then I'd swing the other way, sweating all over the place.

Once I was over, it left me feeling very weak, and the nursing staff later told me that they were very concerned at this stage. The cause seemed to be the infection which had put me in isolation in the first place, because by this time, the wound was beginning to ooze a lot, a fact I was blissfully unaware of until much later. I should also point out that because the incision which had started at my groin, and had gone three quarters round my leg to the back, most of the stitches were out of site, and I was in blissful ignorance because I couldn't see most of what was happening down there.

The chances of losing the leg had just gone up, and I wasn't happy. No Sir, not at all.

Later, Helen told me that of all the time I was in the hospital, this was the time she was the most worried.

The day ended well though. Laura turned up at about four in the afternoon, by which time I was feeling much better, to stay the night. Claire arrived at about six thirty to keep her company in doing the Friday night shift, to give Helen a couple of days at home to rest up a little.

After this morning's little episode, it wasn't easy for her to leave, but necessary nonetheless. We all talked for a while, and then they all went out for a meal together, the girls laughing and chatting. It was amazing given the way they hated each other as teenagers growing up.

<u>Day Twelve.</u>

Things just seem to be getting worse. I have just had a terrible nights' sleep, my temperature is all over the place, and I now have two rampaging infections that seem to be coursing through my veins. The worrying one is obviously the wound infection, but the other has affected my waterworks. It appears that with the recent removal of the amazing catheter, some other nasty little bug has made its' way in though a new entrance, and is thriving, leaving me feeling totally wiped out.

Hopefully, no doubt, I'll pick up in a couple of days, and it won't be so long before I'll be on my way home.

Laura and Claire left at lunchtime; Laura to go back to Manchester, and Claire to go to a party in Lincoln. It's not altogether a bad thing, considering the way I'm feeling at present.

I haven't really been the best of company.

I'm guessing that a big part of feeling down today is that I'd expected to be making more progress by now, and although it seems that the past week is well behind me now, I don't particularly feel that I'm "out of the woods" yet!

I spoke to Helen on the phone, and apparently the Occupational Therapist had been round sorting the house out. This was keeping her busy, not relaxing like she was supposed to be, but doing something practical seemed to be helping her to pick up.
The nursing staff continue to be amazing, if a little strange at times. I've gotten used to the bedpan service. (Ok, it's something you never ever would really get used to, but you learn to accept it…)

229

Tonight choice comment from was from Barbara, a student nurse in her final few weeks, while removing today's bedpan,

"Oh! This is a healthy one. It looks normal….doesn't smell of infection,….smells normal…", all spoken with total enthusiasm in her voice.

These sort of things make me chuckle.

Other than that, there was nothing much happening today to report. Boredom plays a big part in the daily routine, especially at weekends. The time tends to drag, so bringing my own DVD player and DVDs was a very good idea.

<u>Day Thirteen.</u>

I've been here for two weeks now, and I just can't believe it. Where has the time gone? I suppose when you give up time like this, it does sort of disappear. On the other hand, it also has a tendency to stretch out endlessly.

How is that possible?

How can time be so long when it's measured by the second, and then be so short to virtually disappear when we get to weeks?

Although I'd been in the isolation room for only two or three days, it felt like an eternity. It felt like I'd been locked away from the human race forever. Mind you, it looks like were having the worst summer in living memory so I couldn't have picked a better time to be indoors.

If that's not being positive, I don't know what is!

The highlight of today was the daily clean sheets, amazing how good they feel after all these years, and still worth having despite the turning over discomfort which, incidentally, has recently become significantly less painful than the first few days.

But it was time for a downhill turn…
I'd obviously pissed somebody off big time in a previous existence.

The surgeon came in for a chat, and gave me the bad news….

"We're not at all happy with they way the wound is responding to the antibiotics, so we're taking you back to

231

theatre to flush it. This means knocking you out again, sticking in a tube, and draining out the bad stuff".

The antibiotics obviously weren't working and it was all a bit worrying because there was always, on the back of my mind at least, the outside possibility that the leg might just have to go...

I wasn't at all happy at the news because I could still remember the last time I'd been in theatre; it wasn't all that long ago..., and the prospect of the stomach stopping working again was something that I didn't exactly relish, but I did feel a little happier when one of the nursing staff, a little later, told me that the whole thing would be most likely done under a local anesthetic. Like I said...

...I had obviously pissed somebody off big time in a previous life!

She'd got it wrong. It was a general anesthetic, but they did in fact tell me that if all went well, I would only be out for five minutes or so and if things didn't go too well, it would be nearer the half an hour mark.
In actual fact, I was unconscious for over forty minutes, and I am glad to say that it actually went to plan. There wasn't much at all in the way of after effects, with all systems functioning so to speak, and it goes without saying that I was very relieved.

But I knew there wasn't anything to worry about...didn't I?

I was down though, and it took a little while to cheer up again because two weeks away from home is a long time in anyone's book. I was missing my regular hugs and cuddles, and missing those daily emotional fixes I've sort of grown addicted to over the years.

232

I've reached the place in my life where I have forgotten what it is to have the luxury of having the whole bed to myself. It just feels like too much empty space.

Besides, when I sleep in my own, my back gets cold, and given that we're the touchy feely sort of folk, and not used to being kept apart for any length of time any, I wanted to go home... *now!*

To cheer me up even more, I was told later in the day that I'd be at least on the I.V. for two more weeks at least.

I wasn't having a good day.

Day Fourteen

I hate sleeping on my back. It's just so very, very unnatural.

I eventually woke up for the last time at around eight this morning, and felt slightly more human than yesterday. The good news was that it looked like the fever had finally broken, and the waterworks bug had been finally laid to rest.

Today I was once again determined to be optimistic about the day to come. It's a good way to start a day….

I should have known better!

The physiotherapists came around early this morning, and I got dressed in real clothes, for the first time in two weeks. (Ok, it was only into my PJs, but it was my first time out of the hospital gown, and, as I've said before, it's all about little steps at a time.)

Things were indeed looking up, and it was time to get moving.

Claire and Sarah stood either side of me while I got out of bed and stood up, and I immediately felt light headed. I waited a few minutes until my head stopped spinning, *and it was time to take my first steps on crutches.*

I remember thinking that it shouldn't be too difficult, given the amount of crutching I'd done round the village.

Once we'd done two or three steps, I really felt quite comfortable, even though it was a little awkward at first because I was still dragging the I.V. around with me.

We did a "once around the ward", and everyone was really pleased with the way that it was all proceeding…swimmingly.

Claire then asked if I felt up to a stroll outside to the courtyard area which had been renovated into a seating place for patients and visitors and I made it through the doors, and out into the sunshine for the first time.

It felt just brilliant. The Sun was shining down on my face, the air felt cool on my skin and I felt more alive than I'd felt at any time in past two weeks....and this was in Birmingham!!!

I was feeling on top of the world, nothing less than ecstatic and could have stayed out in the courtyard all day. This was real progress...

A yabba dabba doo moment!

The next insignificant test was a simple task and one we take for granted every day, that of standing up in the little boy's room and doing what comes naturally, and don't forget, this little bodily function had been done with a catheter for the first week, and then I'd had to do this little boy thing into a cardboard bottle ever since.

It was another step forward, yet another little step....

Unfortunately, it was a little step too far...

Claire and her colleague had obviously been impressed with the crutching and had left me alone in the toilet, to stand up and do the deed so to speak.

And then came the next setback.

It probably happened while I was turning round, I just don't know, but *my foot went through the floorboards.*

The floor had given way, and whatever was underneath had somehow or other turned to sponge.....bollocks!

Somehow in turning, probably with a big stupid grin on my face because I was feeling totally smug with myself, I'd dislocated my new hip joint....the one other thing that we really didn't want to happen.

A very real... Oh bugger moment....shit!

Shit! Shit! Shit! Shit! Shit!

I collapsed onto the floor, and after realizing that all wasn't well in the "McCourt day out at the toilet", Claire and Sarah came to my rescue and somehow or other, managed to get me into a wheelchair and then back into bed, *and promptly buggered off!*

It was round about now I got very pissed off at Sarah, and wished I'd said something at the time. Walking away, I overheard her saying , "We'll probably get the blame for this, won't we?" Not what I needed to hear at that moment in time.

Inside, I was seething. I recollect thinking along the lines of, *"I know I'm just a patient, a broken piece of meat,....but I'm still a person"*.

Then it was off to X-ray, to confirm what had happened....

I was told soon after that I was scheduled for theatre the following morning, *but until then, I would have to tough it out. I was given a supply of oral morphine to dull the pain, and the waiting game began.*

Looking back, it was difficult to take anything positive out of this particular situation.

It was all bad.

I can honestly say that to begin with, I didn't feel that way. There wasn't much in the way of pain, and I still had a certain amount of movement. I thought that things would be sorted out fairly quickly.

But ever so slowly, things got worse.

Within a couple of hours, I was finding it difficult to lie still, My right side, from my waist down to just above my knee would involuntarily shudder, immediately followed by a deep dull pain which sort of shook until the area settled down again.

It slowly became unbearable.

What was clear was that the original estimate of two to three weeks stay in hospital, had upped and flown straight out of the window, It was time for another mantra, and one, along the lines of, "it's always darkest before the dawn", came to mind.

Mentally, I closed the body down. and tried to relax in such a way that not a muscle in my body would move…..and got used to the idea that this was how it would be for the next twenty four hours.

I sent Helen away, (but she took no notice, and kept coming back.), pointed my eyes on the ceiling and laid still, waiting for tomorrow to come. I'd accepted that tonight I would not sleep because it would only start off another tremor,

But remaining totally still isn't easy, and it just got worse.

Occasionally, I would move my eyes towards the clock in the room to see how many seconds had passed since I'd last looked, but this simple movement of the eyes was sufficient to set off a muscle spasm, and a tremor of pain would ripple down my body.

Occasionally, I would feel an itch on my nose, my face, or my skin, which needed a quick scratch....and another spasm and another ripple of agony would occur.

It was easier not to open my eyes at all.
I'd tried to speak in a way that didn't involve using my facial muscles, but even that would start another event and the grinding of the joint as the two pieces moved past each other during each spasm is something I find difficult to think about even today.

This was my lowest point so far.

The peculiar thing is, that when I look back now, it's as if it never actually happened, the mind once again forgetting what it doesn't want to remember.

It went on like this all night and half the following day, until, at about four in the afternoon of the following day, I was taken to the theatre again.

Earlier that afternoon, the Consultant had been to visit and pointed out, "There's about an eighty percent chance that we'll be able to relocate you without opening you up. There's about a twenty percent chance that opening you up will be necessary, but if that's the case, while were in there, we'll be able to clean out the wound again, so it won't be all bad".

It was nice to know the odds were in my favor....yeah right!

He then put an arrow, with a marker pen, just below my knee, an arrow pointing upwards which said "hip", and left. I started worrying because it was obviously pointing at the wrong place.

Helen thought it hilarious and it was obvious we were once again getting stressed and remember thinking that this last little setback would definitely be my last visit to a dark place.

If all went well, I wouldn't be too far behind schedule for going home.

I was beginning to hate the place,

I eventually went off to theatre, six hours later than planned, and came back to the ward reconnected, and in a very positive frame of mind. Of course I'd been opened up again, and cleaned out again, because it was quite clear in my mind that what was going to go wrong, would go wrong because it was that sort of time in my life.

It happens that way to me, and always has done.

But was I being too critical.

Was I becoming a theatre critic? Well, it was my third visit in just over two weeks...sorry!

Over my short lifespan, I have had many happy moments where I've thought," What good did I do to deserve this?"

But I've also had the opposite moments, the "What the hell did I do wrong for this pile of crap to land on my head".

All my life, my highs are very high highs, but my lows have been usually very low lows, and never ever has my life been on an even keel, so, to me at least, it didn't matter what the doctor said.

It was so, so, obvious, even before I left for the theatre, that in this shitty period in my life, *even a ninety nine percent chance of things going right wasn't going to be enough.*

But it was eventually over and I'd beaten it, again.

I know I keep going on about it, but it was, once again, just time that had passed on by, and, once again, it was in the past. Another little tunnel of darkness, and once again, I'd come out the other end, maybe a little bruised and battered, but more importantly, still spiritually, mentally and emotionally undefeated.

…..but it wasn't quite over just yet!

Days Fifteen to Twenty Two.

I was told I'd need at least a couple of day's bed rest before I could get up and out of bed again, and resume crutching.

I'd been philosophical and accepted that everything that could have gone wrong to date, had indeed gone wrong, and things could only get better, and my positive approach today was to try and find out everything about dislocations so it wouldn't happen again, *and to eat more ice cream, but not the hospital stuff, the good stuff that Helen would bring in.*

It was time to do something and maintain my sanity. I got busy and deleted two hundred and seventy one text messages from my phone, and had a first look at an X-ray of my new pelvis. It wasn't quite what I expected and just seemed so much smaller. It was still quite impressive and I couldn't wait to get it on my computer at home as a screensaver.

But more importantly, I found out round about now that I'd been here long enough to start being Billy again, not to every nurse and doctor, but to some, and it's a start along the road to being me again.

I did have a little crutch around my room because I needed to keep moving forward, but it felt disappointing seeing as I was having to start all over again from scratch.

But the really bad news was that the stomach had stopped working again.

I could now keep on eating, and food was staying down, no chucking up into cardboard trays again, and at least there wouldn't be any aspirations to be done.

But nothing was making its way through my twenty two feet of intestine and out the other end, and so once again I was started on a cycle of suppositories, and laxatives to sort out yet another bout of constipation.

It didn't seem possible, and I was once again heading into a dark place.

It just didn't seem fair.

I was soon in pain again, and in a low, low way emotionally, and found it difficult to cope with even the sound of Claire's laughter on the phone. I was in pain, and very tired.

The stomach cramps came in waves at three minute intervals, and this went on for the next five days. The laxatives and two different types of suppositories hadn't worked yet, and what I'd started referring to as, "the Fylingdales golf ball", just refused to move.

"Are you allergic to peanuts?" asked Laura the nurse, a very enthusiastic lady who was determined to sort me out and just wouldn't give up.

"A strange question to ask", I thought, but the way I was feeling, if she wanted to start shoving a packet of KP nuts up my bum, I wasn't in any state to argue...

"No silly, I've got some peanut oil which worked on another patient of mine.....it's brilliant stuff!"

She administered the wonder oil, but alas, to no avail.

Time once again took on a new meaning and was dragging on once more, The pain was becoming a constant part of my daily life.

242

Our Laura had been here visiting for the weekend, and if I'd spoken more than a couple of sentences to her the whole time, it was more than I remember.

But something strange happened, and I should have expected it.

During my first London marathon, in 2001, I'd reached a low point at about twenty one miles. Everything was hurting and emotionally I was feeling low. As I came round a corner, a band suddenly started playing my favourite Shania Twain song, "Man…I feel like a woman", and from nowhere, I found reserves which I didn't appreciate I had.

Strength came from somewhere, and got me through to the end.

The same thing happened the following year, this time the boost coming from an old friend in the crowd who spotted me at about the same place, and ran alongside me for a couple of hundred yards.

The point is that when we reach a low point, and feel we can't take much more, there are reserves inside each and every one of us which kick in when we need them, and carry us forward, and runners know this, and it makes us stronger. I'd reached a point where I started to feel stronger. I was angry but inside I was saying," Just bring it on because I can take anything you can throw at me".

I started feeling stronger and stronger and knew deep down this particular bout with misery wouldn't beat me and would at some stage be over.

A good thing that happened sometime during these difficult days was being transferred to a bigger room, with en-suite

243

bathroom, and a large balcony, a throw back to the days when the hospital had been used to treat Tuberculosis.

The only down side was that the T.V. didn't have a digibox, but we soon sorted that out. We brought over the one from Helen's room, and stuck it to the T.V. with the gooey tape that nurses put on the cotton wool after they've given you an injection. It was wrapped round and round the digibox, and the TV, about a hundred feet of the stuff, and to begin with, it looked like they'd done a good job.

Unfortunately it was a warm day, and the sticky stuff started to melt.

The digibox slowly started to move downwards, reaching the floor in a little over three hours and I couldn't do a thing to stop it.

Helen and Laura had gone shopping and had missed the entertainment, so I texted them a message to bring back some stronger gaffer tape to put it up again.

They turned up with a ball of string.

Against all the odds, it stayed there for the duration of my stay in Birmingham. So much for health and safety…

The new room was a big improvement. It was cooler, and as summer seemed to have arrived at last, it was really nice to have somewhere to sit out in the sunshine.

But the constipation continued, and on the morning of the sixth day, it was time for the semtex enema.

If this one didn't do the trick, nothing would, and given the amount of laxative I'd taken, I suggested that it was time to evacuate the building.

However, the result was nowhere near as dramatic as it should have been and the blockage started to clear.

Once again, I was amazed at how quickly the body recovers and within hours, I was back in the real world. This time was different though, because I now felt that, because I'd once again come through another setback, I was becoming so much more resilient and knew deep down that if needed, I was ready to fight, and that nothing would beat me.

By tea time and I was up on my crutches again and trying to move forward once more, just round the room to begin with but what was new today was the way I was able to visit the toilet and sit down normally for the first time, albeit with a little help from the nurses, and only possible because of the handrails.

Gravity is a wonderful thing.

It turned out to be a day with a happy ending, because I suppose, everything is relative. I was off and running again, and to top it off, I'd had my hair washed, the drain from my last visit to theatre had been removed, I was in an all round good mood and I had the best night's sleep to date.

<u>Day Twenty Three.</u>

Today, I woke up feeling good with the way the world was going, got cleaned up and dressed, and, putting my best foot forward, I once again, set off crutching up and down the corridor, in much the same way I had crutched up and down the corridor last week.

The difference this time was that I felt much weaker than before; my muscles were trembling, and I had obviously lost yet more fitness through being once more flat on my back for yet another seven days.

Even sitting in the chair was tiring, and I was glad to get back into bed.

At the front of my mind is a definite fear of dislocation, and until I settle down again, this apprehension is going to go on for a while. I've also been told that it won't be until the next three months have passed without incident, and only then, that I can be fairly sure that another dislocation episode will be unlikely.

I'm going to need to be careful.

Mr Grimer came round today and informed me that the bacteria in the wound has now been identified. It's not MRSA, which was my big worry, but I'll need to be on I.V. antibiotics for at least another two weeks, with a further six weeks of tablets, to be sure of getting rid of the infection. Only after this two week period has passed, and if the wound has completely cleared up, would I be allowed to go home. There is no point in taking chances, and besides, it's a long way to come back if anything should go wrong.

I have something realistic at last to aim for. The end of the tunnel seems once again in sight, but honestly, after all the recent setbacks, I'm not holding my breath just yet.

Today, for the first time, I visited the toilet unaided, a major step in the right direction for anyone recovering from an operation like this. This is a big step, and even though I still need to use bottles during the night to pee in. I'm feeling very smug.

It's important to point out that it's a little like being reborn. First of all, you're wiped and cleaned up, as I've been for the past three weeks, like a baby, and I'm now being toilet trained as a toddler.

This isn't something I find easy.

Claire and Carl popped in last night for a fleeting five minutes, on their way to a week's holiday in Newquay. My last thoughts were along the lines of how nice it would be to be there surfing with the pair of them. But not just yet.

<u>Day Twenty Four.</u>

This morning, I was woken up at two-thirty a.m. for the next lot of I.V. antibiotics, and I'm not happy.

What seems to have happened is that I've gotten out of Synch somehow,

These have to be administered every twelve hours and it usually takes between two and a half hours to four hours for the stuff to go in, which means that I'm going to have disturbed nights for at least a week before the timings get back on track. Mind you, it's not as if I'll miss out on sleeping much, it just makes it a little harder.

Unfortunately, the wound is still oozing.

Life has become a regular cycle of twice a day Antibiotics, daily blood tests, and the daily temperature and blood pressure monitoring. A problem which has started is finding a healthy vein to stick the needle in. The Antibiotics they are pumping into me are so strong that they literally destroy the vein, which means that every day, or two days at the most, the needle has to be removed, and put into another vein, sometimes taking up to five or six attempts.

I've noticed that the nurses are better at this than the doctors. What is surprising is how quickly I've gotten used to being poked with needles.
Anyhow, time to cheer up a little. If it's any consolation, if reading this is getting you down, writing it isn't cheering me up a great deal either. I seem to be spending most of my time moaning and complaining about stuff that isn't important.

Bloody hell, I've got rid of the Cancer for God's sake.

Yet here I am whinging and moaning over a bout of constipation and a few days in hospital when compared to many other folks, this is a breeze. My future's looking rosy and it's something I should be thankful for.

At times I'm just a wuss!

And, speaking which, it's time to be thankful for something really important in the recovery of yours truly.

If you recall, I mentioned earlier that, just before the operation I'd been told that there was a fifty percent chance that my sex life would be affected. This was followed by the good news that the operation had been successful, and that this was no longer a problem/

Well, I wasn't all that sure. In fact, given all the setbacks I'd had recently, I wasn't taking anything for granted. It's been a big thing on my mind for quite some time now as I'm sure you'll appreciate.
I won't put too fine a point on it, but during the night, for the first time in what seemed a very long time, *"the flagpole was raised!!!!"*.

It was, however, a bit too early to unfurl the flag, if you catch my drift, so to speak, but I'm taking it as a sign that all will be well in the future.

Tastefully done don't you think?

<u>Day Twenty Five</u>.

I've been told I could be going home next week.

But, before this can happen, I've apparently got some tests to pass.

It's probably another health and safety issue but the physiotherapists have to be happy that I can get about the house adequately on my crutches.

I'd already shown them that I could crutch up and down the corridor without much trouble and this morning I tackled the stairs with my crutches for the first time. By lunchtime, I'd passed all the tests that needed to be passed to allow me to go home.

What was strange was that the physiotherapists didn't bother to tell me.

And here comes the gripe. I know that these guys are busy, and have a lot of patients to get up and moving, but I'm beginning to get a little pissed off at the lack of sensitivity some of the Physiotherapist have to some of their patients. Ok, I mean me.
Maybe I'm still a little angry at the dislocation incident I'm not sure, but it's happened a couple of times since I've been here.
When I had the brace fitted, the strap was too long, and after two days, I got fed up waiting for someone to turn up to alter it as promised, and did the job myself with a pair of scissors. Ok, I know it's only a little thing, but when you're bored out of your skull, they tend to take on bigger proportions.

It would have been nice to have been told I'd passed the tests.

It most certainly would have cheered me up, and I think that sometimes they forget how vulnerable people, yes people, can be at this difficult time. So, a little more sensitivity please….

So, I thought it was time to get my own back. I just couldn't resist it!

My new physiotherapist was a lovely young lady in her early twenties whose name escapes me, and actually she was great.

But I still couldn't resist asking her when I could start up my sex life again even though I'd already had that question answered by the doctor.

She went a lovely pink colour and said she'd didn't know but would go and find out for me, and quickly left the room. To her credit, she was back ten minutes later with the same advice but with one exception.

"Don't be trying out any silly positions! It's not a good idea!"

I was going to ask her to elaborate on the subject but seeing as I've found out that when you reach your fifties, everything you say is taken as totally serious and she might get the idea I'm some sort of pervert, I thought I'd better leave it at that.

Anyhow, back to today, and that word Cancer is back on the menu.

While I've been laid up, Helen has met a number of other inmates whose Cancer stories and prognosis haven't been anywhere near as optimistic as mine, which brings things very much closer to home. She often comes in and tells me about the others who are having a difficult time of things and again, and I realize how lucky I am, in more ways than one.

251

Where we're concerned, if it's at all possible, we seem to have grown closer. What a woman! She's been an absolute angel through all this.

She even brought me curry!

Now, the usual teatime meal was salad. The same salad every night, the only difference being one night it would be corned beef and the next night would be cheese salad, and so on.

The salad bit never changed.
It was half a tomato, some lettuce, four rings of cucumber *and three or four bits of celery!* I'd even tried adding olives and stuffed peppers of my own, and had even got Helen to bring in some Caesar salad dressing to liven it up a little. I was growing to hate salad even more....

Tonight we had an Indian picnic on the balcony.

Once again, I was in heaven. During the day, she'd gone off to Sainsbury's and tonight, we feasted on onion pakoras and curry.

It was memorable and apparently, the smell wafted into every room on the ward and drove them all mad. Mind you, it still wasn't quite the outdoor eating we'd been used to. This is usually the time of year where I would be prancing about in my shorts and tee-shirt, barbequing outside the caravan in the Lakes, or better still, outside the campervan in some beautiful part of Europe, watching the Sun going down over the horizon..

Our only view tonight was a brick wall.

It was memorable.

<u>Day Twenty Six.</u>

I started training again today with a hundred and twenty yard crutch up and down the balcony. It went well.

Unfortunately, to balance things out, the bad news today is that the infections are still running high, and a decision is going to be made fairly soon as to whether or not I will have to go back to theatre early next week, to drain the wound once more.

It depends how it clears up over the next day or so.

To make things worse, the level of antibiotics in my body is too high so the decision has been make to take me off the I.V.s for a couple of days to let things settle down.

I'm beginning to realize how important it is, to leave just a some room in your mind for these little setbacks.

It saves on disappointments later.

I never thought I'd be this pessimistic, but it's also important to remember to grab the positives, and from this little piece of news, the positive bit is that I can now wander freely up and down the ward, and get a clear uninterrupted night's sleep.

<u>Day Twenty Seven.</u>

It's a beautiful sunny morning, and the good news is the oozing is nowhere near as bad as it looked yesterday, so things are looking good for the big inspection in two days time.

My big disappointment today is that it's the first day of the football season, and I'd hoped to be home to watch it on Sky.

I guess it's not supposed to be.

I'm fed up of whinging so much. It seems that's all I've done for days now. Ok, I'm still locked away from other patients in the ward, but so what? For many of these people, their battle is only just starting, their bone cancers being secondary, meaning they may have to face many more months of Chemotherapy and Radiotherapy before they are in a similar position to mine.

And here am I, complaining about a little infection which is slowly coming under control?

The only excuse I can offer is that of being in isolation, where my world consists of nurses, doctors and Helen and the occasional visitor, and the only focus I have had for what seems like months now is me, myself, and me.
No one else.

I needed cheering up. I thought I'd try and embarrass the doctor today.

This was the ward doctor, an African gentleman, and a really, really super bloke.

"I need to ask you an important question!" I whispered over to him while he was doing his rounds, remembering the success I'd had with the Physiotherapist.

"When can I start up my sex life again?"

I swear he blushed! I also swear he went blue!

"Nobody's ever asked me that before!" he sort of sheepishly replied, "I'll find out and let you know!".

"THEY MUST HAVE", I thought to myself,

It's the first question that comes to mind, or it's maybe just me.

Anyhow, the whole thing backfired on me, and I suppose it serves me right. He came back the following day, *and with Helen in the room listening*, gave me the information I was desperate to hear.
"Not until between six and twelve weeks after the operation, and on your back with your legs together!", and off he went back out of the room like a shot.

Now this is the strange bit.

I heard him say, quite clearly I might add, *six weeks* , which to my way of thinking *was really saying three to four weeks*, and given the single bed at home has been fitted with monkey bars, and I've been blessed with a vivid imagination,…not too bad…

So why is it that the only words that Helen heard him say were, *twelve weeks*, and somehow added the words, *at least*, to the end of the sentence.

And when I creatively suggested how the monkey bars could be put to better use, well, in the interest of propriety, it's probably better I don't include what she replied, in case children ever read this.

I've really had a good day today. This afternoon, while Helen was out buying tonight's Chinese picnic, I became independent for the first time by putting on the girdle without help, solo boys visit, without help, and went outside to sit in the big chair, once again without help, where I sat once again feeling very smug.

But, like everything that has happened to be since I arrived here, there is always some bad news. I couldn't believe it. *Happy Larry is back!*

It serves me right for being so bloody smug. *It was probably a bit of payback from the big fella upstairs for winding up the doctor and the young Physiotherapist.*

While I was sitting outside, he came over for a chat.

What could I do? I couldn't exactly tell him to bugger off, could I? Could I?

It was another reason for me to get home as quickly as possible.

He didn't recognize me at first, and the conversation started off being actually being quite pleasant,

However, it was soon fairly obvious that the bloke wasn't having a good time. He was actually struggling, because unfortunately, his infections hadn't cleared up after months of treatment, and it was likely he was in for another knee replacement.

He could be an inmate for at least another six weeks. Bugger!

I felt a bit bad wishing his leg would fall off....I had to bite my tongue though, when he came out with, "I didn't want to say anything to put you off, when we last spoke, about the operation I mean, because *things could have gone wrong*! *They sometimes do you know?*"

It seems that this had been Happy Larry's way of being positive. The guy is amazing!.

Day Twenty Eight.

I'm blaming Happy Larry for today's bit of news. It's probably my own fault though. I think the Gods upstairs have got it in for me. I think it's retribution for wishing his leg had fallen off, or maybe it was for winding up the hospital staff. The bad news today is that the wound is now seeping worse than yesterday, most likely because I'd come off the antibiotics.

I'm resigned to the fact that another visit to the theatre is inevitable.

It's a bit of a downer really, but they've already told me that I won't be released until they're satisfied it's properly sorted. Before I go down to theatre, I intend spending the day taking every laxative known to man.

I'm taking no chances.

Terry and Jill came visiting this afternoon and this has cheered me up no end. I also cheered up because I'd realized that whilst I couldn't watch the football on Sky, I can still get Match of The Day, and thoroughly enjoyed Stevie Gerrard's winning free kick against Aston Villa, even though a draw would have been a more honest result. I could also wind up a couple of the nurses who were big Villa supporters. Seriously though, these Liverpool games are important because me, and the girls text each other throughout the game when something good has taken place. Laura is a fanatical Liverpool supporter.

To cheer me up even more, Claire and Carl landed tonight, on their way back from their holiday in Newquay, *and brought me a "dirty old man" walking stick.*

It's got a mirror on the end of it, designed to look up ladies skirts, or Scotsmen's kilts if you're a woman. Maybe it should be renamed a "dirty old person's" stick, seeing as how we're all terrified of being anything other than politically correct.

I suppose I'd better not use it at school though.

In the very politically correct world of Education, it's probably a sacking offence.

<u>Day Twenty Nine.</u>

It's the start of my fifth week in Hospital, and I've had enough.

Enough is enough and I want my life back.

I've taken everything that they could throw at me and have responded to it all as cheerfully and politely as is possible. I've been jabbed a thousand times and am now running out of veins, and it feels like it's time to go home.

What's worse is that I've eaten the same salad for tea, every night for five weeks, (except for the curry night, and ok, the Chinese night), and despite adding my own olives, peppers and salad dressings, I'm beginning to dread tea time.

It's time to go home when you know the fortnightly hospital menu off by heart. I would miss the puddings and custard though.

So why am I so cheerful?

I'm hungry, and I've been kept on nil by mouth since midnight last night.

I need to go home and recover properly. Don't get me wrong, I understand the importance of making sure that everything is sorted before I leave because if it's not quite right, it's a long way to come back, and what could happen is quite serious. It's been a necessary chunk of my time that I've lost, and I realize I've been looked after by some extraordinary people.
But it's time to be me again, and I want to go home.

I feel that I've slowly built up enough strength and confidence to cope with the challenge of living in a house again, away

260

from the controlled environment of the ward, and I want to go home to Helen, and the kids.

Is this loud and clear?

At midday today, I got the good news that a return visit to the theatre isn't needed, the oozing is slowing down and drying up....and I can have some lunch.

It's good news, but nothing really has changed. The wound still hasn't healed enough for anyone to be really satisfied, I'm back on I.V. antibiotics, and the cycle continues. It's now just a waiting game.

But it is going in the right direction and we're on the run in.

This is hard, because it's all about being patient, and patience has never been one of my virtues. Today, time just dragged, on and on and on.

Day Thirty.

Today is the day that Helen is deciding whether to leave me.

To go or not to go, that is the question.

It's time for her to go home, and with luck I won't be too far behind. She's been living in the nurse's hostel forever, and it's time for her to go home, and get ready for a new school term. I'm on the mend, and am at a stage where I can look after myself. Well sort of…

I decided to make the decision easier for her by sorting myself out big time, this morning, washing myself down completely, shaving, being spick and span for when she arrived.

She was impressed, and so was I. What is surprising are they ways you learn how to do things, just by being innovative. I'll explain later.

But I have reached the little boy stage…baby…toddler…now little boy because I can now clean myself up in the mornings and get dressed. We're getting there slowly.

I'm now up to crutching one hundred and twenty yards, three times a day, with three lots of exercises, in between the hook ups, so were starting to get there slowly.

……Helen went home at Six tonight, and although I'll miss her terribly, she needed to. This whole thing has been hard on me, but doubly so for her, always being in a position where you feel helpless to do anything. I don't want her to go but that's just me being selfish. She also needs to go home to make sure the house has been sorted for my homecoming, whenever that will be…..the food, the band, the table dancers…as if I were that lucky.

262

It's more about banister rails.

I really didn't want her to go home to an empty house, so I phoned Claire up to make sure there was at least a bottle of milk in the fridge when she got there. When she got there, surprise, surprise, her Mum and Dad were also waiting, as well as Carl and Claire, and I believe a party sparked up.

She's been amazing in a way that fills me with both humility and gratitude.

Even so, I deserve it!!!!

<u>Day Thirty One.</u>

Today I got released into the ward. The infection was still there, but we're winning, and I'd been allowed to go up and down the ward for a change of scenery. What it really meant was that I could now talk with other patients and see what I'd been missing.

Today I met Liz. She's been recovering in the room two down from mine and had had her leg amputated just below the knee, early last Thursday. It's now six days later, and she's bombing up and down the ward in a wheelchair and she decided to come a visiting. (She'd smelled the curry earlier and was curious...)

It's amazing what progress she's made in that short time, and seems confident about the future. She did mention she'd had a weepy day yesterday, which confirms what I've been saying about it being normal to have off days, as long as we dig deep and bounce back. She also mentioned the shadow pains which were troubling her. I could only give her my "edging forward one step at a time mantra", and the taking the positives bit. I've no doubts we'll talk again.

I've also started doing laps of the ward, and it was encouraging. Being so long in isolation, I'd forgotten what a positive effect other people can have on your own progress, and just stopping for a chat was a real tonic.

It was also nice for Claire the Physiotherapist to fondle my bum. Ok, not my bum, more like my upper thigh, just below my bum, but it was quite nice nevertheless. She reckoned she was checking out the muscle deterioration, but I like to think differently.....

Helen had spent the day with the Occupational Therapist putting the final touches to the house. It won't be long now....

Day Thirty Three.

It's a very sad day today. Malcolm died.

Malcolm, and his wife Betty are friends of Helen's mum, and the last I'd seen of him was when David the Horse Whisperer did his thing. He'd been battling with Cancer for quite a while now and hadn't looked well at all.

He'd finally lost his fight. I know Betty will miss him.

It once again brings the word Cancer back to the forefront of the mind. My world continues to turn. The wound is still oozing, so it's the same old story, hook up, exercise, hook up, exercise and sleep.

I met Mick today. Mick's another marathon runner who had run London the same year I did, and he makes number three. The long distance runners I've met since being here, I mean, and it's funny how the mind works, but I started wondering if there was any connection. I've heard the Cancer attacks where it's weakest, and in a runner, at the point where he or she is completely knackered…..well, it got me wondering…

I've just had my stitches out, and it's definite that I won't be going home this weekend. I'll still be here for the next four or five days when the next ward round is due. Time to be philosophical again….I'm a little disappointed, but now that I'm social again, and seeing just how fortunate I really am, a couple of days more doesn't seem very much to be making a fuss about.

Robin came visiting today, and cheered me up. Robin is the third member of the "Last of the Summer Wine", sad lads on bikes, team who tackled the Tourmalet, a couple of summers ago. This was quite an achievement as we'd done it to celebrate his 60th birthday, and Lance Armstrong calls it "the Ballbuster", the toughest climb in the "Tour de France".

He's the one who made it all the way down safely.

We've done a lot of miles together and he's kicked off my enthusiasm to make sure we do a lot more next year.

<u>Day Thirty Four.</u>

It's Friday today, and it's been definitely confirmed that I'll be here until next Tuesday at the very earliest. What's been strange is now that I'm out and about, how many people have disappeared from their beds and actually gone home in the last few days. It's infuriating that I'm still here, *and all because of a lousy little infection.*

Today, the good news is that I'm now off the I.V.s, and only need to continue with oral medication. More little steps in the right direction.

You'll also have noticed that for quite a while now, I haven't added in any more stories lately. It's as though real time is on hold, if that make sense. It's as if all of my past life has become insignificant right now, and my future life is on hold until I get over this period of present.

It's maybe just waiting for me to become me again, before I can write some more about me again. Well, it makes sense to me…

Even though I know that I'm close to going home, I'm still having to dig deep again, because it's as if now that I've got over the big setbacks, I can relax a little, but experience has told me that these are the times that stuff goes wrong when you least expect it. I've started to let my guard down, so it's time to toughen up again. Being totally honest, a quick crutch around the ward and a chat with some of the other patients soon brings things back into perspective, and the blues slowly wander away….

I've just found out that Helen's coming back down again tomorrow. I think maybe I shouldn't have told her about Claire

268

the physiotherapist feeling up my bum, she's always been the jealous type.

<u>Day Thirty Five.</u>

The wound is now looking definitely better. I'm getting even more frustrated.

I'm doing well with the exercises and I've also worked out a way of walking with the crutches which is much faster than the way I've been normally getting around, so I'll check it out with the physiotherapists to make sure I'm not doing any damage.....

Helen arrived at lunchtime and looks so much better for spending a little time at home. The house is ready for my release, and she's so much more positive in herself.

I hadn't realized how much I've missed her.

We had another picnic on the balcony, consisting of some Salmon Terrines as starters, Chinese food for main course, and some Mango smoothies to wash it all down.

The Sun set over our brick wall, and in honesty, it would have been hard to find a nicer setting. I guess we're the sort of people who are nauseatingly happy together no matter where we are. (I'll be glad to get home because I'm beginning to sound like Barbara Cartland, all gushy and mushy and soft....)

<u>Day Thirty Six.</u>

I've been really spoiled today. I've had both my legs washed and my hair washed, the first time in over a week.

I would never have thought that soap and water could cheer you up so.

The crutching is going really well, and I'm holding myself back a little with the new technique. I'm not seeing a physiotherapist until tomorrow.

Today I spent mostly watching T.V. and reading. I'm simply passing time now, as best I can.

Helen went home at Six tonight and I spent the rest of the night watching more movies on the DVD player. Not long now....

<u>Day Thirty Seven.</u>

A major slice of luck came my way today. About time too!

Mr Grimer did his rounds a day early, and I've got the nod to finally go home on Wednesday. It could have been tomorrow, but unfortunately, Wednesday is the earliest that they can book an ambulance to take me there. Time for a Fred moment…"Yabba Dabba Dooooooo".

These are things I've been told to look out for though. I've been told that I must not get into a car for a couple of weeks at least, due to dislocations, and for the first three months after the operation date, not to travel anywhere in a car for longer that fifteen minutes, because I might not get out of it again.

So Wednesday it is.

To be really honest though, I thought I'd be a lot more overjoyed than I am. It's hard to explain.

I think it's because deep down, I'm scared of another last minute relapse, but maybe it's also because, although I'm going home and that's great, it's not going to be the same home that it was when I left.

It's not at all about the chair raisers, or the handrails, or any other paraphernalia that's been added since I got here. I think it's about how I'm going to cope around the place, especially during those first few days.
I've made good progress here, but the point is, it's all been in a carefully controlled environment. I've had people to depend on, and my worry is about how much I am dependent on anyone else. I've had a visit from a few thoughts, like, "how will I get the milk out of the fridge?", or "how will I put my socks on?"

272

It's all a bit topsy turvy right now and, in the bigger picture, nothing that I won't beat with time. I suppose it's really quite normal to be thinking this way.

Where I'm going, although it's my home and is very familiar, it's become almost alien territory now, at least for the first couple of days.

It's silly, I know, because it'll be great to see everyone again, especially as I'm going home on our Claire's birthday, and I can't think of a better excuse sit down and eat some real Indian curry.

<u>Day Thirty Eight.</u>

Today had been a very long and worrying day.

I got out of bed this morning and on my first lap of the ward, my calf muscle didn't feel right. My leg is swollen from the knee downwards and it's giving me a whole lot of discomfort. I've quickly decided that I'm taking no chances and intend spending the whole day in bed, in the hope that it settles down quickly.
The consultant had a quick look, and he seemed fairly satisfied that it's not a lot to worry about, but I'm taking no chances.

I'm learning fast that when it comes to diagnosing my medical problems, the one person who knows when something isn't quite right is me.

And something isn't quite right.

The lack of exercise today has left me with no appetite tonight, but seeing as its salad again, I'm not exactly brokenhearted over the matter. I decided to pig out on chocolate instead.

I'm going home tomorrow, and I'm twitchy. This is despite another visit from Robin to cheer me up, and finding out that Claire has bought me the new Liverpool shirt.

<u>Day Thirty Nine.</u>

I woke up this morning and thought to myself, "Bugger it!"

My calf and knee are still swollen, so I decided to put my brace on, and try and walk it off. It worked on my bike earlier in the year, so I thought, "why not give it a try?"

After ten minutes or so, crutching up and down the corridor, it had noticeably eased off, making me feel a little more reassured.

Today I'm going home!

I must be excited because I'm cleaned up, dressed, packed, I've exercised, and am ready to go home, *and it's only six forty five in the morning.*

I've been too wound up about the leg, and too excited about going home to get much sleep, so I got stuck in early, and am pleased with myself, in a little boy sort of way, that I've managed to get everything done without any help.

It's another step move. Here I am, all dressed up, and nowhere to go...at least not just yet.

It looks like it's going to be a long morning.
Actually, the waiting wasn't too bad. I spent a lot of the time saying my goodbyes to Mick and a few other patients on the ward, promising to keep in touch, and then said my goodbyes and thanks to the doctors and nursing staff of Ward 12, who have simply been amazing.

Given how each and every one of them had wiped my bottom at some time during the past five and half weeks, I wondered

*what it would be like if one day, we met up in a pub
somewhere, and had a drink together?*

It's a nice idea.

The two ambulance drivers arrived at midday, and off we went
home, me lying down in the bed in the back, The second lady
driver sat in the back with me all the way, and because we
chatted almost non stop, the three hour drive home went by
very quickly.

I remember thinking afterwards, "These guys were good". I'd
hardly noticed the journey. My only disappointment was that
I'd expected a "bee bah ambulance" with sirens and flashing
lights, and this was more like a minibus with a bed in the back.

Never mind.

Getting home was brilliant.
I walked up into the house, through the garage, and noticed for
the first time the new garage doors that Helen's dad had had
fitted so I could get in and out of the house easier. I went
through into the living room, very carefully because all the
floors in the house had a different feel to them than the rubber
non-slip hospital floor I'd gotten accustomed to. I'd also
noticed the single bed in the dining room where I'd be
sleeping for a couple of weeks at least.

Heading upstairs to my own bed was strictly no no, for the
foreseeable future, or so I was told.

It was time for a good cup of Yorkshire tea.

My calf was still swollen, if anything it was worse than
yesterday, but I'd learned to be more careful over the last few

weeks, and so decided to spend the rest of the day in bed, in the dining room to let it settle.

The rest of the evening was great. We celebrated Claire's birthday, with me flat on my back, eating curry and restricting myself to the one tin of beer. Eddie and Marilyn also came round, Eddie with his nose red because he'd been out to somewhere near Whitby, for a few pints of beer with an old friend.

To cap it all, I watched England get beaten by Germany, again, although the word watched may not be the right one. From the top of my head in the dining room, to the little T.V. at the back of the conservatory, the distance must be about thirty feet, too far away to see anything clearly on a 15" screen, so I didn't exactly see the whole match, only the close ups.

I more or less heard England get beaten by Germany....again. but not on penalties, so maybe it wasn't too bad.

We'd had a really nice night, and I was really, really, really, glad to be home.

....What a shame it lasted less than twenty four hours.......you'd think that I'd been through enough, and it was all hunky dory from now on in, but unfortunately, the Gods above had decided to have a little more fun at my expense, another setback was just around the corner, another sting in the tail......bugger!.....time out....

By now, you must be thinking what a moaning bugger I've turned into and I'm thinking you are probably right. My "Me and my Cancer" book, has turned into, "How I moaned and whined while I got over an operation" book. It's no big deal and lots of people have had similar periods in life where they're laid up for a few weeks. I think the difficult bit for me was learning I'd become disabled and my life would be changed forever. I don't want to be disabled and don't know how well I'll cope with it. It's not the "how I got rid of Cancer in three weeks" nonsense, it's more about not being able to do all the things in life that make me who I am. Only time will tell.

<u>Day Forty….and beyond.</u>

If you're waiting for the happy ending, it comes later… I hope.
The God's hadn't quite finished playing with me yet. There
was still one final sting in the tail…. and this on my first night
home.

During the night, the swelling in my leg had continued to ache
no matter how much I tried to move it, and I'd woken up to
find my foot laying on it's side, not a good sign. I gingerly slid
my leg over the side of the bed, and gently tried to stand up. It
was time for another oh bugger moment….bugger, shit,
bollocks, and any other swear word I could remember.

The floor was spongy…. again.

It had dislocated…..again!.

"Why me?"

It's just not fair….*and my first thoughts were, "how do I tell
Helen?"*

Yes, you could say I was a bit pissed off!
I phoned Birmingham who said to get an X-ray done to
confirm things, and we'd take it from there. Three hours later,
I was sitting up in bed in Scarborough Hospital, It's a good job
I hadn't unpacked I thought to myself.

I did however get my "bee bah ambulance" ride.

Strangely enough, it wasn't all that exciting. Maybe it was
because I just wasn't in the right sort of mood to enjoy it!

Sometime later, the orthopedic consultant came round and
confirmed the bad news, also saying *he'd never seen an X-ray*

quite like it, but they'd try to pop it back in the following morning. He also said that it looked like I'd probably need to be opened up again which sent the alarm bells ringing. Very loud ringing, clanging from one ear to the other...

The anesthetist came round later that night confirming I'd be first one down in the morning, and *he'd also never seen an X-ray quite like it...*

I felt like a bit of a celebrity.

I settled myself down and waited for the dreaded muscle spasms to start up, fully expecting to have yet another night of misery, but lo and behold, they never came.

It was obviously not as bad a dislocation as before.

Helen wasn't at all happy when she heard the news about going down to theatre the following morning. She tossed and turned all night worrying about what would happen, and decided to phone Birmingham herself.

Both the Surgeon and the Anesthetist came round early the following morning to explain what would be happening, and I can honestly say I was fairly happy about the whole thing. I just wanted it put back in again, so I could go home.

About an hour later, it was all change again.

Birmingham had contacted the Scarborough lot and told them that this type of relocation wasn't the sort of stuff they were used to, a different format to the usual hip replacement set up.

"Don't do anything, and send him back to us", was the message, loud and clear, and I thought that was that.

I was gutted. I'd really, really, really, had enough of the salads down there,

I just wanted to go home......I was fairly devastated.....

And out of the blue, just when I least expected it, the miracle happened. Ok not quite a miracle, that's just me being dramatic, but it was close, and for me, right now, this was up there with the best of them.

Dr Bakhir walked in....the same Dr Bakhir who had been my anesthetist in Birmingham, and the guy who had diagnosed what was wrong with me in the first place.

"What are you doing here?" I asked, the optimism very evident in the tone of my voice.

"I'm up here working, and saw your name on the operation list. There can't be too many William McCourts, can there?" he replied, or words to that effect.

To make this bit short, he went straight back down to the Orthopedic department, sorted things out with the people down there, and agreed to put me back together (I'm starting to sound like Humpty Dumpty...all the kings men etc.....), again, under the proviso that if I did in fact need opening up, it would be straight to Birmingham.

Of course I agreed. What had I got to lose?

I took him less than three minutes.
I was knocked out once more, and my first question on waking up was, "How long have I been out for?" The fear of my stomach stopping working again was there in large amounts, and I'd had no time to load up with laxatives.

"Three minutes mate", was the reply. I was elated. The man was a hero. I wanted his picture on my wall to worship…if I could have his children…Ok, not quite, but I'm hoping that you can see how happy and delirious I was.

I didn't have to eat more salad, and, about an hour later, and I was tucking into a hearty lunch, somewhere near the top of the world.

I was told I'd need two weeks bed rest, and then it was back down to Birmingham for reassessment.

I did in fact only did spend five days in the hospital in Scarborough, because I mentioned that I'd already been six weeks away from home, and there was nothing being done in the hospital that couldn't be done at home. I asked if I could spend the rest of the time at home, where I'd be a good boy and stay in bed, as per the doctors orders.

Helen had agreed to doing the bedpan bit…yuk!

 Isn't love wonderful?
I promised to do the same for her some day, but she didn't seem all that excited….some days you just can't win.

"What's going to happen when I get down to Birmingham?" I asked the consultant when he came on his rounds.

"It's quite probable that you'll have to have it done again…..it shouldn't have dislocated as easily as that", he replied, and this didn't cheer me up one bit.

"What's going to happen when I get down to Birmingham?", I asked his colleague, the other consultant, when he did the rounds the following day, because I didn't much like the first answer…

"It's unlikely they'll do it again, unlike a normal hip replacement, there isn't much pelvis left to work with. There's always stuff that can be fixed on to it, to stop it from coming out again…", he answered.

It was fairly obvious that nobody was quite sure what would happen, the procedure I'd had was all too new.

And I started wearing white Lycra…

Not the full superman outfit, cape and all, that would have been weird. I was just wearing white Lycra stockings to stop deep vein thrombosis, but in a funny sort of way, *I'd actually become "White Lycra Man", and I suddenly knew that things were going to be ok!*

I know it sounds stupid, and maybe I was grabbing at straws, but when I mentioned this to Helen, she knew exactly what I meant. We'd had a good laugh at Claire's White Lycra Man vision, in the nicest way of course, but you had to give it to her, she'd been right.

I then spent the next seven days in bed at home, which had been moved to the front living room where I could both watch Sky TV, and see the view of the sea from my front window. I've got to admit, it was a bit disappointing being flat on my back again, but somehow it was very different this time. I just knew I was over the worst. I really did know. I deep down knew this part of the journey was nearly over.

I went down to Birmingham the following week, all packed for another long stay, but that wasn't the case at all. The decision in Birmingham was easy. Do nothing, let things heal up, see what happens and come back in a month's time for a week of intensive Physiotherapy.

Two days later, I was home again, and it was time to let the healing begin.

Part Three. Where we are today.

Which sort of brings me up to where I am today, four months further on, and mending very nicely, thank you very much. I'm not sure if I'm now Billy McCourt, victim of Cancer, or Billy McCourt, Cancer survivor? Or the bloke who lives at the end of the street with the limp.

I suppose that's up to me!

It's January 2008, we've just put Xmas, and a bloody awful 2007 behind us, *and I've just seen Kylie.*

She's been in this years Xmas Dr Who and I thought she looked great.

Ok, she seemed to look a little older and a little more tired than the last time, but it's hardly surprising is it?

To me at least, she still looks fantastic.

The last few months haven't been easy, but since I donned the white Lycra stockings, there have been no setbacks. I've learned however to slow things down a little, and never say never again.
Because of my roller coaster journey of setbacks, I know that somewhere inside me is a little box containing my emotional survival kit, to be opened if times get hard again, because I'm very much aware that setbacks can come along anytime.

I'm hoping I'll never have to open it again.

The first thing that I think it's important to point out is that my world is a much slower place than before. Things take a lot longer to do, and not a lot seems to get done in a day, but bit by bit, it's starting to pick up pace.

September was very much about starting again, which saw me out in the street every day, crutching between lamp posts to try and build up strength. After two weeks, I could get to the end of the street, and by the end of the month, I could make it down to my mother in laws on the next street.

Once again I was accosted by little old ladies and geriatrics on their invalid Harley Davidsons.

My world had started to expand a little. The only setback during the month was the sodding scaffolding.
Some builders had come to fix the roof which had been damaged in last winter's storms, and when they put the scaffold up, they blocked the signal to my Sky dish….bastards.
October was a breakthrough month, during which I'd gone back down to Birmingham for a week of intensive Physiotherapy. This was brilliant, and this time the Physiotherapists were brilliant. It was a week of Gym sessions which almost killed me, and two sessions a day in the Hydrotherapy pool. I was still on two crutches when I went in, and when I came out I was down to one. This meant I now had a spare free hand, and could do so much more around the house.

By the end of October I could get in and out of the front door, could crutch to the other end of the village, avoiding well meaning pensioners, and catch a train into Scarborough, where I'd have a little walk around, and then come home again. I have to admit though, it was quite hard going, and I slept a great deal afterwards.

But it was progress.
The real sign of progress was that I could now take Helen her morning cup of tea in bed, which has been so important in making marriage work in our house.

Without her morning cup of tea, life isn't worth living...

By the end of this month, I had started driving again, not too far, and not for too long, but a move forward nevertheless. What helped was changing our saloon car for a small people carrier, which made getting in and out that much easier because the driving seat was higher.
I'd also reached the stage where I could have a shower again down at the mother in law's, instead of the regular wash down at the bathroom sink, which was another boost to the old confidence. And, by using my crutch upside down, a shoe horn and the hand grab, I found I could put my socks on. Ok, I couldn't tie my laces, but I could stuff them down the sides of my shoes.

But best of all, I could get upstairs to sleep in my own bed again, and snuggling and cuddling were the norm once more. I also found that I could make it to the toilet if needed, in the middle of the night and out went the plastic bottles......

October was a good month.

By the end of November, I made more progress, but is seemed the rate it was happening was slowing down.
Some things were getting back to normal. For instance, I could get dressed fairly quickly now, could fasten my shoe laces instead of tucking them down the side of my shoes, I could drive for longer distances, and I could bend over and pick stuff up off the ground.

I could also get into the bath at home to have a shower, but the big happening this month was that I could now sleep a little on my good side, and not have to keep on sleeping on my back, which I just never got used to.

It was also important to me that the house was starting to get back to normal as well. The big upright chair with the chair raisers went, and we got the living room back to normal. The single bed in the dining room was long gone, as were the tall stools in the bathroom and kitchen I'd been given to help me get around.

The raisers and support frames around the toilet seat, as well as the nasty plastic extension I'd had to sit on, all went away this month as well. Apart from a couple of small handrails, the house was now pretty much back to the way it was before.

December was brilliant!

For the first week in December, I went on a trip round Germany with Helen's brother, Tim, who visits a dozen or so companies in a five day period, as part of his job in the family business. This was my first big test to date, my first big challenge, and involved having to deal with four different hotel rooms and two nights on the North Sea Ferry, both nights in a force eight or nine storm. These were new alien environments, and I looked on the week as a bit of a benchmark to see how I could manage, and to really see where I was up to with the progress I'd made..

The week went swimmingly, and I'm very grateful for the patience that Tim showed all week. When we set off, I was bombarded with sentences which were along the lines of, "Are you alright?", "Can you manage?", and "Can I carry that for you?". By the end of the week, we'd gotten way past that, and I found myself crutching backwards and forwards from our seats, to the bar to get my round in, all the while the ship was rolling from side to side. I did cope well, but it's still very much like I said earlier, my world is a much slower place than before.

We ate well, we drank well, and we laughed a lot. It boosted my confidence immeasurably.

My next adventure was the week before Xmas, when I drove over to Whitehaven to drop off Xmas presents, and see many of the family for the first time since the diagnosis.

A week earlier, I had met a new friend, Amanda Roberts originally from Whitehaven, and now living in Canada who was also an acorn, from a different branch of the family tree, and who was also an author.

With our Colin, that made three of us. (Ok, I know. I know I'm not an author yet, not until I finish this book, but give me a chance!)

She had had a book published recently called "104 men" about the William Pit Disaster of 1947. in Whitehaven and has a website dedicated to the mining community. I came across her website quite by chance and read the following.

Dedication

In the early spring of 1847, in a churchyard far from the town of his birth, the body of a coal miner was laid to rest in an unmarked grave. Whether anyone present truly mourned his passing, only the crows can bear witness. But of this I am certain, he had been a man worth knowing.

I have his song to sing, a haunting sweet anthem that speaks of the life of a man, and of the many others who accompanied him in an age long ago.

I dedicate this site, its content, and the passion that burns in the heart of its creator, to the honour and memory of:

THOMAS UNTHANK
Pitman from Whitehaven
1788-1847

I found it very moving.

Thomas Unthank, the man in the dedication, was on of my ancestors.

The point is, my trip to Whitehaven started with an email from Amanda telling me where Thomas was buried, and on my way over to Whitehaven, I decided to have a look at the churchyard where he was laid to rest in a pauper's grave.

I found the whole experience very moving.

It was a cold and overcast winters day, and the church looked hauntingly beautiful, What made it all the more lovely was the sound of a children's choir, practicing Xmas carols, as I walked towards it and I immediately thought of my old Granddad, and of us singing together in the choir all those years ago.

Thomas's brother, John, my great (x7) grandfather, had also been killed in a pit disaster, in Whitehaven, way back in 1819. I think it's sufficient to say at this stage, that Thomas had been a bit of a brilliant bloke in his time, and I want to find out more about him.

I finally caught up with Colin.

We spent a night and a morning going over the history of the McCourt family in Whitehaven, and the family tree was now starting to take shape. I had a few surprises.

Colin was also a big Thomas fan, and he informed me that, *Thomas could read and write,* which in those days was unheard of. Most of the other miners signed for their wages with an X, but not Thomas.

But the amazing thing for me was the fact that Thomas, a miner all those years ago, and an acorn from way far back in the family tree, *had also written a book!*

His brother's death had obviously affected him, and he'd spent a great part of his life writing letters to many influential people of the time. This also included letters to Parliament, all on the subject of mine safety. He eventually produced a book on the subject and because of this, and other letter's he'd written, he'd been jailed as some sort of radical. He was jailed on more than one occasion, and eventually was forced to leave Whitehaven with his wife and family, to walk to just outside Sunderland, the other side of the Country, where he later died.

Colin and I have already decided that sometime next year, we will do "Unthank's Walk"

While I was over in Whitehaven, I visited the street where the three brothers who had been killed, had lived, and suddenly remembered going to Cubs in a building situated in that very same street. I visited the place where John had died almost two hundred years before and realized I used to play not fifty yards away as a small boy.

I visited the Haig Mining Museum, which is now situated in an old boiler house, at what was Haig Pit, and the memories

291

came flooding back once more. It was the same old boiler house my Granddad used to take me in when I was a small boy. It was next to the room where the men would go up and down the mine in the cage,

...and there on the wall in front of me, was the marriage certificate of one Samuel McCourt and one Elizabeth Unthank. Thomas Unthank's niece.

I visited my mother for the first time in a couple of years because I have to say that her support throughout this time has been unwavering. Maybe it's not too late...

To close this little reminiscence, the weather for those few days in Whitehaven had been outstandingly beautiful, a very white frost which stayed all day, and a spectacularly clear, blue, sunny sky. It seemed appropriate that the weather had done its' part in making these few days so memorable.

It rounded things off nicely.

What's more, Christmas this year was simply fantastic.

The day before Christmas Eve, we all went to the Church Carol Service, where I bumped into Jeff again. We sang our hearts out, but I was a little dismayed to find out that someone had changed the words to some of the Carols. I mean, what's wrong with Latin? Over in the pub later, the carol singers turned up, and we sang the proper words so all was well once again.

We had a meal on Christmas Eve with all the family, in a local pub, where we chatted, sang and danced until the early hours. Laura, and I did our party piece on the karaoke, "A Fairytale of New York", and I'd managed to get all the way through without getting choked up. For reasons I can't quite get my head round, I've been more emotional than ever this year, welling up at the least little thing. I've never ever managed to watch Bing Crosby's, "White Christmas", without an eyeful of tears, and this year, I was worse than ever.

Another piece of good news was that *my dancing had significantly improved*, according to the Mother-in-Law, and I also found out that the crutch made an amazing air guitar. I had problems doing the Hokey Cokey, with all that "put your right leg in and shaking it about" nonsense, but I reckon my rock and rolling was second to none.

Christmas day found sixteen of us round the table and we had the best Christmas ever!

Helen had worked incredibly hard to make it so, and after the year that we'd gone through it seemed only right that we had a good one.

Carl set us off on a new tradition this year. He presented the family with a large wooden plaque entitled, "McCourt's Outstanding Achievement of the Year.", and each year from now on, we would honour the best achievement from someone in the family with a little silver shield with their name on it, and what they'd done to deserve it.
For some reason, I'd been awarded this years silver shield, though I couldn't see why?

But he has no idea how competitive I am, and that I fully intend winning it every year from now.

Amazingly, I still managed to get a couple of golfing accessories as presents, as I do every year. Thankfully, some things never change. Mind you, Helen did point out that there's no reason I can't be playing again in 2008. After all, it's all about being positive.

January meant another visit to Birmingham for yet another week of Physiotherapy, and once again, I'm moving forward nicely. I have to admit, I found it hard to walk through the doors to Ward 12 again, because it brought back such vivid memories, but it was actually brilliant. It was time to give a little back in that I had a chance to talk to people who were now where I'd been a few months before.

The hugs from the nurses were also very nice.

Most importantly, it was also time for my first check up, and although I'd had a couple of sleepless nights of needless worry, the tests all came back clear. Lance Armstrong wrote that these regular Cancer checkups are always a difficult time. It's when the "What if?" demons come out to play.

So, where does that leave us today?

I now realize that where the Cancer is concerned, that part of the journey is more or less behind me, but, in other ways, there is another journey that has only really just begun. I have to think about the future, about going back to work and getting on with life. I'm almost ready for it, but not just yet!

My journey into the family history will continue, if for no other reason than to meet more lovely people. I fully intend to keep climbing higher into the family tree, give it a shake, and see what falls out. I would very much like to know a great deal more about the last days of the brothers, find out more about Thomas Unthank, *and I haven't even touched the surface of the Venezuelan family.*

294

I have to accept that my running days are now over, but I haven't given up on the cycling. I've just bought a new, girls bike, and no, it's not pink, and no, it doesn't have a basket on the front... I can't get my leg over the crossbar on a man's bike.

But I can get my leg over.....

I have a feeling that there is yet another adventure that needs to be planned, and maybe at some future date, embarked upon. Me, and my geriatric mates are thinking about cycling to Spain next year to raise a little money for one of the Cancer charities. We're going to call ourselves S.L.O.B.S, short for "Sad Lads On Bikes", because our Claire reckons the sight of old codgers like us, prancing about in Lycra is very, very sad.

I really do like the idea.

I'm also planning to do the "Unthank Way", sometime later in the year, tracing the route across the north of England that Thomas took all those years ago. I have already enlisted the help of some map specialists to work out the highways and byways he would have walked upon, and maybe we can raise a little more money for a worthwhile cause. If I can't walk that far, I'll do it on my bike...but I will do it.

The real positive outcome from all of this, despite all the ups and downs, is that we're even more together as a family. We really are one big happy family. And that's great.

I know I've moaned and whined a lot, but deep down, I know how incredibly lucky I've been just to be here to write this book, many people haven't been quite so fortunate. Through all this, I've learned that not only myself, but all of us are very much stronger than we realize, and inside each and every one of us is a strength we often don't realize we possess. It just needs tapping into.

I hope someday, somebody reads this account of my experiences with Cancer and can get something positive out of it because being positive is a major factor in beating it, It's been good for me to write it.

Cheers.